Take a STEP

How to Have Tax Free Retirement Income for Life

STEP:

The Strategic Tax-free Evaluation Process for Keeping Your Future Income Out of Uncle Sam's Pocket...and Back Into Yours!

By Joe RoosEvans

CFP, CTFA, RICP, AEP, CLU, CASL, CLF, CAPP, ChFC, MBA, WMCP

Contents

Dedication

This book is dedicated to my father, the person who taught me how to live life with passion, insight, and determination. And to my beautiful wife, Lori, who makes every day worth living; and to my son, Aidan, whose spirit and promise inspires me to be a better father. And finally, to every family everywhere, no matter where you are on the road to your dreams. May you savor the joys of a rich and tasty life!

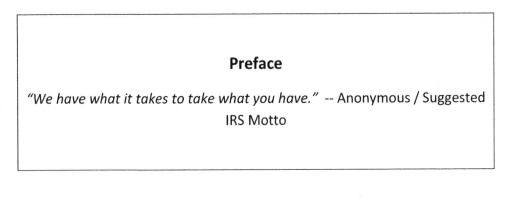

Preface

"We have what it takes to take what you have." -- Anonymous / Suggested IRS Motto

What if I told you that, after all the years you've saved, invested, and planned for your retirement, you would have to hand over up to half – or possibly even much more – of your future income to Uncle Sam?

Not a pretty picture, is it?

But unfortunately, this scenario is much more probable than you might think. And because of that, most people will be shocked to learn that when they've finally reached the "finish line" in their working lives, the government could be the primary recipient of their retirement income, pension benefits, and yes, possibly even your Social Security.

In fact, the better your investments have performed over the years, and the more income you generate in retirement, the more Uncle Sam likes it, because he – not you - will be the one who is reaping a good share of the reward.

By the time you reach retirement, it might be too late to do anything to change this scenario. So, those who haven't planned ahead for this legalized highway robbery are usually stuck. This, in turn, can cause a significant impact in how you are able to spend the remainder of your time on this earth.

But it doesn't have to be that way. *Read on!*

There's a big financial storm on the horizon – one that could literally decimate the retirement income that you have available to spend. But there are ways that you can prepare for it – and in doing so, you can ensure that you are able to spend 100% of the future income you generate...regardless of what the future income tax rates are.

On top of that, you can also keep your hard-earned money safe in any economic environment, while at the same time, knowing that those you love will be financially secure – both now and long into the future.

So, why should you listen to me as you go through this journey?

Hopefully, my humble beginning will provide some inspiration...as the son of immigrant parents in a blue-collar neighborhood who ultimately has become the CEO of a national financial services firm.

I have been financially secure for many years. But, for me, success was never about "the money." It was more about earning a winning sense of achievement, from the satisfaction of leaving behind a well-mowed lawn when I was eight years old, to astounding myself and others after winning more than 20 AMA motorcycle racing championships.

I was a young man then and thought I had it all, but I was just getting started – soon to become a four-time competitor in the national "Mr. America" body-building championship, placing as high as fourth in the nation while in my 40's.

But the *real* triumph came later, after I discovered my most powerful gift – the ability to teach others how to build financially successful lives and seize the finest trophy that anyone can have: a secure and prosperous financial future...without the burden of excessive taxation.

Are you ready to learn how you can possibly move yourself and those you care about into the 0% tax bracket?

Just turn the page and let's get started!

About the Author

Joe RoosEvans is one of the top financial experts in the country. He started in the wealth services industry in 1982, and after several very rewarding years, he founded Financial Resources of America (FRA). Ranked among the Top Five Percent of wealth service agencies in the world today - a leading force in the industry since 1986 - FRA is one of a group of several successful companies founded by Joe RoosEvans - all of which continue to further his reputation for leadership and innovation nationwide.

Over the years, FRA has served more than 17,000 clients who have come to Joe and his company for advice on how to best preserve their wealth. Today, the company and trust company manage over $4 billion dollars in assets.

This accomplishment is largely the net-result of Joe's passion and commitment for serving people in a quest for successful retirement lifestyles. Joe has committed his entire career to helping individuals create, grow, and protect their wealth.

All told, Joe RoosEvans is a widely recognized leader in wealth preservation, and in the financial services industry overall. An acknowledged wealth expert, radio talk show host, author, and sought-after national speaker, his professional designations include the following:

- Certified Trust and Financial Advisor (CTFA)
- Certified Financial Planner (CFP)
- Chartered Financial Consultant (ChFC)
- Chartered Life Underwriter (CLU)
- Retirement Income Certified Professional (RICP)
- Accredited Estate Planner (AEP)
- Certified Wealth Preservation Planner (CWPP)

- Certified Asset Protection Planner (CAPP)
- Chartered Advisor for Senior Living (CASL)
- Chartered Leadership Fellow (CLF)
- Wealth Management Certified Planner (WMCP)

Clients who rely on Joe RoosEvans and FRA know that they are working with well-established and experienced professionals in the wealth protection and preservation field whose sole purpose is to help them reach their goals.

Joe RoosEvans isn't your cookie-cutter financial guru. He is an innovator, educator and a passionate advocate of financial literacy, for everyone...everywhere. He is also supportive and generous, as the founder of Support Our Heroes, a charity that will benefit from every sale of this.

His very active family includes wife, Lori, and son, Aidan, who follows in Dad's footsteps as a motorcycle racing champion. By age 10, Aidan had won 14 National titles on motorcycles, before turning to 4-wheels. By age 14, he won numerous championships and rookie of the year awards in Karting, Open Wheel Micro, Midgets, and 360 Sprint Cars...and Aidan is just getting started. Joe's hobbies, after spending time with his family and being an active member of his church, include studying and always asking "Why" and "Why not?"

Joe is the author of several books that educate investors and retirees on how to generate tax-free income, and to transfer assets seamlessly by avoiding probate and reducing – or even eliminating – Uncle Sam's portion. You can find all of Joe's books on Amazon by visiting: https://www.amazon.com and then typing Joseph RoosEvans into the search bar.

FRA

As a company that specializes in estate and income planning, FRA is committed to excellence, and the latest planning tools, so that its clients won't have to risk experimentation on their own.

For multiple generations of family members, as well as for individuals, FRA places a key focus on legacy strategies, which includes specialized trusts and long-range tax-reduction tools for beneficiaries in order to provide a plan that works in harmony with specific income and wealth preservation goals.

The FRA family of companies has more than three decades of experience in assisting families with protecting and better controlling their wealth. Since FRA was founded, the company has grown to become a leading authority in all aspects of income and estate planning. FRA regularly delivers high-profile seminars across the United States, where experts share their advice for maximizing the value of individuals' and families' estates in order to benefit them during their lifetime, as well as to benefit their loved ones thereafter.

FRA is able to provide income and estate planning, as well as legal and financial services, all in one complete package. You can find additional information on FRA and the services they provide by visiting: www.FRATrust.com.

Introduction: Will Uncle Sam Be the Biggest Beneficiary of Your Retirement Income?

"The difference between death and taxes is death doesn't get worse every time Congress meets." -- Will Rogers

It has often been said that, "the only constant in life is change." And for the most part, that is true. Think about how different your life is today than it was twenty, ten, or even just a few short years ago.

Unlike years ago, there are likely a long list of potential scenarios that keep you awake at night, too, such as:

- Outliving your savings
- Declining health
- Remaining independent
- Not having anything left to leave your loved ones

A somewhat similar list of worries holds true for the United States as a whole – particularly as it pertains to the debt it is racking up. According to Bloomberg, the U.S. deficit is growing even faster than initially anticipated. In fact, the U.S. government ended fiscal year 2019 with a deficit of $984 billion – the largest in seven years, and the first time since the 1980s that the budget gap has widened over four consecutive years.[1]

Although numbers like that may not be alarming to you personally, they should be, because paying down these debts will fall to the U.S. taxpayers like me and you!

How exactly will this happen?

Primarily by way of the good old-fashioned income tax. And if you think you're paying a lot in taxes now, just wait, because it's expected to get much worse.

Are You Racking Up an IOU to the IRS?

Do you know what income taxes will be next year? In 5 years, 10 years, or in 20 years?

Probably not! In fact, no one does.

But if you did, planning financially for the future would be a whole lot easier.

What we do know is that the U.S. income tax brackets have literally been all over the board throughout the past century - with the top bracket even exceeding 90% in some years.

If you are currently in the top income tax bracket, you may think that the government has its hands on a significant portion of your income. But the reality is that, over the past decade or so, the U.S. has been experiencing a historically low tax environment.

But just wait. This won't last forever. And given the fact that we're gearing up for a financial storm, your retirement income could be on shaky ground.

So, if you don't know what your tax rate will be in the future, how will you know if you'll have enough net income to fund your lifestyle in retirement?

The answer is - you don't...unless you take control of your future income out of Uncle Sam's hands and put it squarely into your own.

That's just what this book is all about. By following the strategies you'll learn here, you can literally – and legally – take yourself out of the "tax zone," and possibly move into the 0% bracket.

So, why wait like a sitting duck for the government to dictate how much of YOUR money they're going to take?

By using our exclusive STEP plan (Strategic Tax-free Evaluation Process), I'll show you exactly how you can get around this tax hurdle, and how you can take control of your retirement income and keep more - much more - of it in your own pocket...because your financial future depends on it. And it's never too early to do something about it.

Sources

1. U.S. government's annual budget deficit largest since 2012. By Lindsay
   Dunsmuir. Reuters. https://www.reuters.com/article/us-usa-economy-budget/u-
   s-governments-annual-budget-deficit-largest-since-2012-idUSKBN1X426T.
   Accessed December 26, 2019.

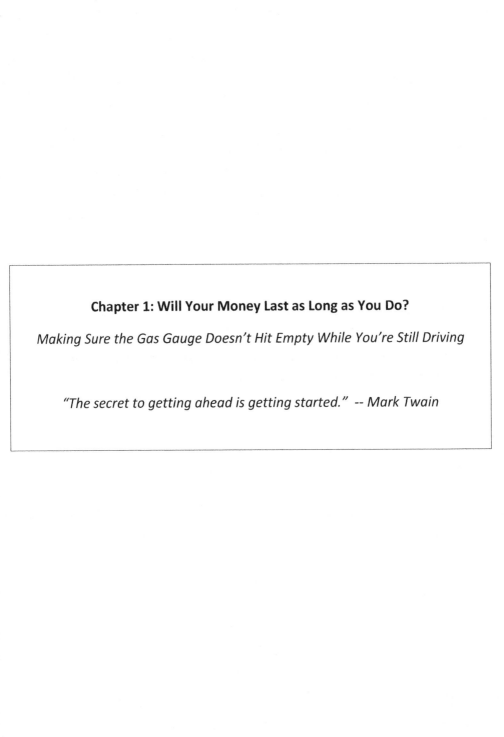

Chapter 1: Will Your Money Last as Long as You Do?

Making Sure the Gas Gauge Doesn't Hit Empty While You're Still Driving

"The secret to getting ahead is getting started." -- Mark Twain

On the road of life, there are any number of "potholes" and other obstacles that can slow your trip down, or even require you to cancel your plans altogether if you run out of gas.

The same holds true when it comes to your savings and investments, and particularly your retirement income. Without a good solid income plan in place, it's likely that once you retire, you'll be watching your savings (i.e., the "gas" that keeps your financial motor running) dwindle until you run out.

Then what?

More and more retirees today are having to rely on loved ones in order to just get by. Older workers in retail stores and fast food restaurants are becoming the norm now, versus the exception, for generating needed income.

There is a long list of road blocks that could derail your financial future. These can include taxes, rising living expenses, health care costs, and a possible long-term care need. Some of these are within your control, and others are not.

But even so, you can still plan ahead for them financially. That, in turn, can make your entire trip much easier, and more predictable.

Will Your Retirement Road Be Rocky?

Although people are living much longer these days (on average), this can actually be a challenge, because if you live a nice long life, you need to ensure that you have an income stream that matches your time frame.

So, unless you know the exact day and date that you'll be exiting the earth, it just makes sense to plan for the worst – just in case - which, in this scenario, is having more time.

But simply planning your income based on a longer life is just the beginning. That's because there are many, many ways that your income can be siphoned off, which in turn, makes the amount you have available for your living expenses less...and given the probability of higher taxes in the future, what you actually net in your pocket could be miniscule.

The Day Has Finally Come

While you might think that your retirement will never get here, eventually we will all say goodbye to our employer or to a business that we've worked years to build – either on our own terms, or on someone else's. But once you leave the security of a regular paycheck, there are differing scenarios that could represent the next phase of your life.

Take James, for instance. He and his wife Mary had just celebrated their 40th wedding anniversary when suddenly Mary suffered a stroke. Leaving her cognitively impaired and paralyzed on one side, her long-term prognosis was not good.

After two months in the hospital, Mary was finally able to come home – but only with the aid of an in-home care provider. Without any type of long-term care insurance in place, James paid approximately $5,000 per month for Mary's home health aide – which required James to deplete the couple's emergency fund, and to then start dipping into their retirement savings.

Unfortunately, six months after her initial stroke, Mary had another, and she ultimately passed away. And, because James only had life insurance on himself through his employer, he ended up having to pay roughly $10,000 out-of-pocket for Mary's funeral and other final expenses.

Because the couple traveled extensively in their younger days, they didn't really get around to building up a substantial retirement fund for their future. On top of that, the great recession of 2008 diminished their wealth even more...and they still hadn't gotten back to even, more than a decade later.

So, when James was forced to take early retirement at age 62, his options were somewhat limited. He knew that he could start drawing on his Social Security benefits – which currently equaled $1,807 per month.

James' friends and coworkers warned him that by starting his Social Security income benefits early, the dollar amount would be permanently reduced. This, in turn, would end up drastically reducing his total amount of income for the remainder of his lifetime...or would it?

Waiting a few more years, when his full Social Security benefit at age 66 would be more than $2,500 per month, was one option that James considered. But, as it turned out, waiting for a higher income amount from Social Security would not be the best alternative for him. In fact, James learned that starting Social Security benefits at age 62 is oftentimes the most lucrative alternative for many retirees.

Ultimately, in order to save on expenses, James temporarily moved into the spare bedroom at his son and daughter-in-law's home. And, while James is happy to see his two grandsons every day, this is not at all the retirement that James had envisioned.

To make matters worse, James' son has recently been offered a great job in another city. If he takes it, James will have to make alternate housing arrangements...or move to a different area of the country that is hundreds of miles away from his friends, his doctors and other professionals, and essentially his comfort zone.

And, while the option of staying put and living on his own would definitely stretch James' budget right now, the possibility of rising taxes, along with inflation, in the future would further reduce his available income – and his independence - even more.

Who could he rely on then?

So given his situation, James decided to meet with a wealth expert to discuss his possible options. He was amazed at what he learned, and he was immediately able to put a plan into action.

Potential Lifetime Social Security Benefits Based on Age

Age	Age 62	Age 66+	Age 70
60	$1,807.00	$2,542.00	$3,239.00
61			
62	$21,684.00		
63	$43,368.00		
64	$65,052.00		
65	$86,736.00		
66	$108,420.00		
67	$130,104.00	$30,504.00	
68	$151,788.00	$61,008.00	
69	$173,472.00	$91,512.00	
70	$195,156.00	$122,016.00	$38,868.00
71	$216,840.00	$152,520.00	$77,736.00
72	$238,524.00	$183,024.00	$116,604.00
73	$260,208.00	$213,528.00	$155,472.00
74	$281,892.00	$244,032.00	$194,340.00
75	$303,576.00	$274,536.00	$233,208.00
76	$325,260.00	$305,040.00	$272,076.00
77	$346,944.00	$335,544.00	$310,944.00
78	$368,628.00	$366,048.00	$349,812.00
79	$390,312.00	$396,552.00	$388,680.00
80	$411,996.00	$427,056.00	$427,548.00
81	$433,680.00	$457,560.00	$466,416.00
82	$455,364.00	$488,064.00	$505,284.00
83	$477,048.00	$518,568.00	$544,152.00
84	$498,732.00	$549,072.00	$583,020.00
85	$520,416.00	$579,576.00	$621,888.00
86	$542,100.00	$610,080.00	$660,756.00
87	$563,784.00	$640,584.00	$699,624.00
88	$585,468.00	$671,088.00	$738,492.00
89	$607,152.00	$701,592.00	$777,360.00
90	**$628,836.00**	**$732,096.00**	**$816,228.00**
91	$650,520.00	$762,600.00	$855,096.00
92	$672,204.00	$793,104.00	$893,964.00
93	$693,888.00	$823,608.00	$932,832.00
94	$715,572.00	$854,112.00	$971,700.00
95	$737,256.00	$884,616.00	$1,010,568.00
96	$758,940.00	$915,120.00	$1,049,436.00
97	$780,624.00	$945,624.00	$1,088,304.00
98	$802,308.00	$976,128.00	$1,127,172.00
99	$823,992.00	$1,006,632.00	$1,166,040.00
100	$845,676.00	$1,037,136.00	$1,204,908.00
101	$867,360.00	$1,067,640.00	$1,243,776.00
102	$889,044.00	$1,098,144.00	$1,282,644.00
103	$910,728.00	$1,128,648.00	$1,321,512.00
104	$932,412.00	$1,159,152.00	$1,360,380.00
105	$954,096.00	$1,189,656.00	$1,399,248.00
106	$975,780.00	$1,220,160.00	$1,438,116.00
107	$997,464.00	$1,250,664.00	$1,476,984.00
108	$1,019,148.00	$1,281,168.00	$1,515,852.00
109	$1,040,832.00	$1,311,672.00	$1,554,720.00
110	$1,062,516.00	$1,342,176.00	$1,593,588.00

After discussing James' financial concerns, his advisor showed him how much he could earn throughout the years by starting his Social Security income at certain ages, with a primary emphasis on taking this income now at age 62 and investing it. Because James was currently living with his son, his expenses were minimal – so he had time to generate more savings while watching his money grow.

In this case, the advisor recommended that James start taking his benefits right away at age 62. Then, by investing that money and earning 5%, James would be able to build up a significant amount, even over just a few short years.

Estimated Growth of James' Invested Social Security Income

Age	Age 62 Int	Age 66+ Int	Age 70 Int
60	5.00%	5.00%	5.00%
62	$22,768.20		
70	$240,701.88	$133,241.66	$40,811.40
75	$427,021.16	$338,607.73	$266,857.07
80	$664,817.02	$600,712.66	$555,355.00
90	$1,355,655.89	$1,362,173.66	$1,393,492.30

Disclaimer: The dollar figures may vary, based on the amount of monthly Social Security income received, as well as rate of return. Consult a professional retirement income specialist for more details based on your specific information and objectives.

His advisor went on to show James just how much more he could accumulate by investing his Social Security income benefits over time, versus simply receiving the monthly income and then spending it.

Social Security Income Received versus Invested Over Time

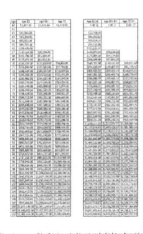

This put James on a solid path to increasing his nest egg for his future financial needs.

Taking it even a step further, James' advisor showed him a way that he could grow his money on a tax-deferred basis (and unlike a traditional IRA or 401k plan, continue to make contributions past age 72), while at the same time ensuring that his son, daughter-in-law, and grandchildren will inherit a nice sum when James passes away.

This could be done by purchasing a cash value life insurance policy, using James' $1,807 per month from Social Security to pay the premium. On top of that, depending on how James decided to pay the insurance premium, he could have paid-up coverage within just a few short years.

As an example, based on James' age and health, he could purchase a policy at age 62, and immediately secure a death benefit of $370,000, while stopping his premium payments after just 8 years. Alternatively, if James decided to continue funding the policy for life, the policy's face amount – or death benefit – would increase to $463,000.

James' advisor also showed him some other options, too, for the sake of comparison, which outlined how much coverage could be purchased if James waited longer to take his Social Security retirement benefits.

For instance, if James waited until age 66 to start receiving his Social Security, his monthly retirement income benefit would grow to $2,542 – and if James used that money to purchase a policy, the coverage of more than $200,000 could be paid up in just four years. (Coverage of more than $500,000 could be obtained if James paid the premiums for the remainder of his life).

Similarly, if James waited until he was age 70 to start receiving his Social Security income, his monthly payment of $3,239 would get him roughly $550,000, with a premium that is payable for just ten years. Likewise, if James decided to pay the premium for the rest of his lifetime, the policy's face amount would grow to $650,000.

James felt that this strategy was a great way to get a tax-advantaged return on his money, as well as a benefit down the road that his loved ones could use for paying off their mortgage, funding the boys' college expenses, or any other need that they choose.

Some of the funds from the life insurance policy's death benefit could also be used for paying James' future funeral and other final expenses. This would alleviate a great deal of financial stress for his son when the time comes.

Plus, because the policies have "living benefits" – a method of accessing a portion of the death benefit while the insured is still alive – James would easily be able to pay for his care if he eventually required home health care assistance, or if he needed to move into a nursing facility once he was qualified.

The bottom line is that James now had several viable options that he didn't realize he had until he met with a professional wealth advisor who was able to customize a plan that closely met James' needs – both now and in the future. James also had more control over his financial security, regardless of what happens with taxes, inflation, and other possible risks to his security.

After considering all of his potential options, James ultimately chose to begin taking his Social Security income immediately, using the income as a funding mechanism for a wide range of other financial possibilities both for himself, and for those he cares about.

In the meantime, Linda, one of James' close friends, also recently lost her spouse, Michael. Although Linda and Michael didn't accompany James and Mary on many of their travel excursions, the two couples did enjoy going out to dinner and a movie at least once each month.

Following a lengthy battle with cancer, Linda's husband Michael passed away. But thankfully, due to a combination of long-term care insurance and several income-producing investments, Linda was able to keep her husband at home, where he was the most comfortable, until the very end.

Linda is age 62 now, and eligible to start drawing on her Social Security benefits. She initially had plans to wait until at least age 69 or 70 to begin taking this income, so that the dollar amount of the benefit would be increased.

But after hearing about the plan that James' financial advisor had set up, Linda decided to start taking her Social Security income right away, too – even though she didn't really need it for paying her monthly living expenses – so that it could be invested and grow over time.

Following the loss of Michael, Linda had also decided to remain in the home that they shared for many years together. And, because she is bringing in more than her expense obligations each month, Linda has been able to take her grandchildren on several nice trips to the Gulf of Mexico, as well as set up a college savings plan for each of the grandkids.

In addition, because many of Linda's other retirement income streams are coming from tax-advantaged accounts like her Roth IRA and loans from her life insurance cash value, Linda will be able to count on a set amount of income, regardless of what Uncle Sam decides to do down the road in term of tax increases.

While both James and Linda had very different financial situations, both were able to move closer to their desired retirement by taking advantage of solutions that they didn't previously know were available to them.

With that in mind, regardless of whether or not you start planning your retirement early, the good news is that you could still have some attractive financial options. But in order to put these strategies in place, it requires taking action now rather than later.

Will You Be Dependent or Independent in Retirement?

Given our longer life expectancy today, the number one fear on the minds of retirees, as well as on those who are preparing for retirement, is running out of money before running out of time.

Even if you've been a good saver all of your life, inflation and rising taxes could literally decimate the amount of income and assets that you have available for YOU, as well as those you would like to leave something to.

One income method that many retirees have relied on for a number of years is the "safe" withdrawal strategy. This consists of "drawing down" one's portfolio – which typically consists of roughly 50% stocks and 50% bonds – and using the funds for income, while the remainder of the money stays in the portfolio to generate growth...hopefully.

(Because a "safe" rate of return was initially thought to be 4% per year, this strategy is often referred to as the 4% Rule).

But unfortunately, this retirement income generation method just simply doesn't work today. This is due in large part to the combination of an extremely volatile stock market, as well as historically low interest rates. In fact, there are many "assumptions" made regarding this strategy that can render the 4% rule unsafe, and ultimately, as a road that leads straight to a depleted portfolio.

In fact, today, the new "rule" pertaining to a "safe" withdrawal rate has fallen from 4% to between 2.2% - 2.8%, depending on the asset allocation. So, this, too, depends on where your money is invested. Given that, while you may be able to "stretch" your income out for a longer period of time, just the opposite is true as well, in that your portfolio could deplete more quickly. Because of that, it is essential that you talk with a retirement income and estate preservation specialist in order to create the right asset mix for you and your specific objectives.

How Long Will Your Money Last with 40% Equities?

		40% Equity Allocation					
		Retirement Period (Years)					
		15	**20**	**25**	**30**	**35**	**40**
Probability of Success	**99%**	4.4%	3.1%	2.5%	2.0%	1.7%	1.5%
	95%	5.1%	3.8%	3.0%	2.5%	2.1%	1.9%
	90%	5.5%	4.1%	3.3%	2.8%	2.4%	2.1%
	80%	6.0%	4.5%	3.7%	3.1%	2.8%	2.5%
	50%	7.0%	5.5%	4.5%	4.0%	3.5%	3.2%

Source: Morningstar

In this case, for instance, based on the chart above, the probability of the portfolio lasting for 35 years – if you withdraw 2.4% per year – is 90%. And with that, the money that you withdraw may be reduced by taxes. If you are drawing 2.4% from a $1 million portfolio, you would end up with $24,000 pre-tax ($1,000,000 X 2.4%), but even less after Uncle Sam gets his portion.

So, even with a portfolio that consists of only 40% equities (for the reduction of risk), the probability of success over time diminishes – and it is reduced even further each year. This means that your money could run out while you still need it.

For example, the reciprocal of the initial withdrawal rate of a portfolio is the amount you would have to have saved in order to reach your income goal. Here, for instance, if you wanted a 4% initial withdrawal rate, you would need a portfolio that was 25 times (1/4% = 25) the annual income that you desire in retirement.

Alternatively, if the initial withdrawal rate decreases to 3%, then the amount that you must save in order to withdraw the same dollar amount decreases, too. Then, the amount that you must save in order to withdraw the same annual dollar amount as in the 4% example would increase to 33.33 times the target income amount.

Likewise, giving yourself a "raise" in order to help keep pace with rising inflation can wipe away your portfolio in the event of a market "correction." And, while you could withdraw less income each year to help make up for this, there is still no guarantee that your money will last over time – or that you'll have enough to pay your expenses in the future.

Even reducing the equity portion of the portfolio down to 20%, primarily for the purpose of reducing market risk, can render the possibility of your portfolio running out even further.

Here, for instance, while your money will likely be "safe" from market volatility, going this route has also reduced the opportunity for added growth. This equates to less purchasing power over time.

That being the case, you may need to cut out various expenses in retirement, move to more affordable housing (or move in with a loved one), and / or skimp on necessities like health care and prescription medication.

How Long Will Your Money Last with Only 20% in Equities?

20% Equity Allocation						
		Retirement Period (Years)				
		15	20	25	30	35	40
Probability of Success	99%	5.1%	3.8%	3.1%	2.6%	2.2%	1.9%
	95%	5.6%	4.2%	3.4%	2.8%	2.4%	2.2%
	90%	5.8%	4.4%	3.5%	3.0%	2.6%	2.3%
	80%	6.1%	4.6%	3.7%	3.2%	2.8%	2.5%
	50%	6.6%	5.1%	4.2%	3.6%	3.2%	2.9%

Source: Morningstar

Disclaimer: The probability of success may vary, based on the performance of the portfolio. Consult a professional retirement income specialist for more details based on your specific information and objectives.

Similar to the example above, if you were drawing down 2.6% of a $1 million portfolio each year, then your $26,000 annual income could still be subject to taxation – essentially netting you less (and depending on what the future income tax rates are, it could be quite a bit less). Here, the probability of success – in other words, the probability of your portfolio lasting for 35 years – would be 90%. So, while 90% may seem like good "odds" at a casino or a racetrack, do you really want to take the 10% chance that you may run out of money before running out of time in retirement?

There is a better way, however, to ensure that you not only have income that will last as long as you need it – but also that your money is safe (and growing). This means that you can sleep easier, knowing that no matter what the income tax rates are in the future, you won't be liable for providing Uncle Sam his cut.

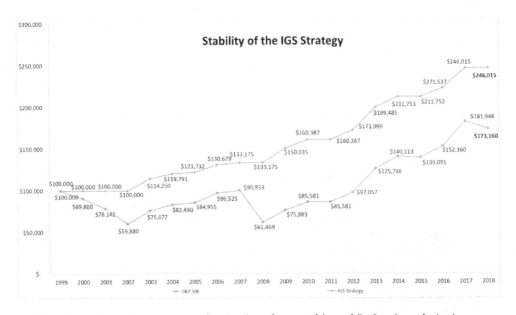

Stability of the IGS Strategy

Disclaimer: The probability of success may vary, based on the performance of the portfolio. Consult a professional retirement income specialist for more details based on your specific information and objectives.

In fact, regardless of how much you have actually saved, getting your hands on the money that you need will typically require that you find a way to "bypass" Uncle Sam's portion altogether. That's because in retirement, income is much more important than net worth.

The following chapters in this book will show you just how much financial danger may be lurking around your future income, as well as provide strategies that you can implement and take control of the wheel, ensuring that your gas gauge stays full for the whole trip!

Chapter 1 Key Takeaways

- There are numerous risks to your money, including inflation, taxes, volatility, and a future health or long-term care need. But the biggest risk is longevity, because living longer subjects you to all of these risks for a longer period of time.
- Taking Social Security retirement benefits at age 62 – even at a reduced dollar figure – can be more beneficial than waiting to draw at your full retirement age.
- "Traditional" retirement income strategies like the 4% Rule no longer work in today's volatile market and low interest rate environment.

Chapter 1 Action Steps

- Determine how much you will receive from Social Security at age 62.
- Determine your approximate monthly expenses in retirement – including what you may need to pay in income tax on your investment, pension, and / or Social Security income. (In other words, how much you will actually "net" and be able to use towards paying your living expenses?)

Chapter 1 Questions to Consider

1. True or False: Reducing the equity portion of your portfolio to reduce risk could actually lead to your money running out sooner.

2. Taking your Social Security retirement benefits at _____ can allow you to invest it for a longer period of time.
   a. Age 62
   b. Full retirement age
   c. Age 70
   d. None of the Above

3. True or False: Most retirees can count on a defined benefit pension plan to last throughout their lifetime.

4. The biggest risk(s) to your savings include which of the following:
   a. Inflation
   b. Taxes
   c. Living longer
   d. All of the Above

5. In the past, a "safe" rate of withdrawal was usually _____ percent.
   a. 4
   b. 14
   c. 40
   d. 50

Chapter 1 Answers

1. True. Reducing the equity portion of your portfolio to reduce risk could actually lead to your money running out sooner. This is due primarily to low returns, as well as the inability to beat – or even meet – inflation.

2. Taking your Social Security retirement benefits age 62 can allow you to invest it for a longer period of time.

3. False. Most retirees are not able to rely on defined benefit pension plans because most employers have done away with these types of plans. One primary reason for this is the expense of the employer paying out income to retirees for a long period of time.

4. The biggest risks to your savings include inflation, taxes, and living a longer life (as your money will have to last for a longer period of time).

5. In the past, a "safe" rate of withdrawal was usually 4 percent. This income strategy is oftentimes referred to as the 4% Rule.

Chapter 2: Board Up! A Big Financial Storm is Coming

Don't Get Caught Without a Lifeboat

"The financial crisis should not become an excuse to raise taxes, which would only undermine the economic growth required to regain our strength." -- George W. Bush

If you opened up your credit card statement and saw a chart like the one below, you would likely consider cutting up your card (or at least you should!) This is actually an estimate of the U.S. budget deficit...and it isn't a pretty picture. In fact, it's anticipated that the deficit is growing at a much faster rate than initially estimated.

Federal Government Expenditures

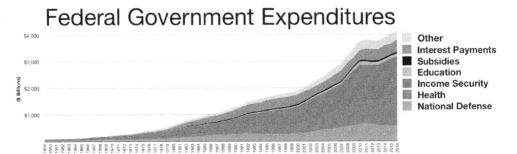

https://en.wikipedia.org/wiki/Expenditures_in_the_United_States_federal_budget#/media/File:US_Federal_Government_expenditures.png

In addition to the budget deficit, the government's debt is also skyrocketing. As of this writing, the U.S. National Debt stands at roughly $23,152,299,850,000.[1]

Why should you care so much about these figures?

One reason is because you, me, and everyone else who lives in the U.S. is on the hook for helping to pay it back!

If you divide that total figure out so that we all pay our "fair share," the Federal debt per person in the United States is approximately $70,000.[2] But this doesn't even include state and local debt.

Nor does it include the "unfunded liabilities" of entitlement programs like Medicare and Social Security. The fiscal strain on just these two programs alone could bankrupt the United States. These debt "responsibilities" can also make your personal share quite a bit higher.

According to the Congressional Budget Office if Social Security, Medicare, and Medicaid go unchanged, the rate for the lowest tax bracket could increase to 25%, and the highest bracket could shoot up to 88%.

If you don't think this can happen, all you have to do is take a look back in time, because the federal income tax bracket in the United States has already had years where that figure has been surpassed!

Brace Yourself for the Coming Financial Storm

Depending on how much you've saved, along with your timeframe and anticipated future living expenses, you are likely working to retire sooner or later. But regardless of when and where you retire, one thing is for sure - and that is you will have to pay tax on your retirement income.

Although many financial professionals will tell you that you'll be in a lower tax bracket in retirement, that is not necessarily always the case. In fact, in some instances, depending on how much you are bringing in from various income sources, your tax bracket during retirement may even be higher than it was in your working years.

With that in mind, it's important that you not just take the word of a traditional financial planner, because making this type of assumption could end up costing you dearly.

While we don't know what the income tax rates will be years down the road, we do know that they are much more likely to go up than they are to go down. This, in turn, could have a substantial impact on your future income, your lifestyle, and your life overall.

Unfortunately, following most of the "traditional" rules of saving for the future – such as setting aside money in tax-deferred plans like a 401(k) and traditional IRA – may actually do you more harm that good.

Sure, you can deduct your contributions into these types of plans. But keep in mind that, when it comes to the U.S. government, there is no such thing as a "free lunch." So, while it might seem like they're doing you a big favor by allowing pre-tax contributions, and a deferral of taxes on gains over time, the reality is that Uncle Sam is really just waiting to take a larger slice of the pie – *your* pie - down the road.

In addition to that, when you come to the proverbial "end of the road" here on earth, Uncle Sam may very well be your biggest beneficiary, too. So, based on the planning you do right now, your loved ones could end up with only a small percentage of what you intended. All of this is leading us right into a financial storm.

What exactly is driving the financial storm that's on the horizon?

There are actually several key components. One is the massive group of Baby Boomers, the first of whom started turning age 62 in 2008, which qualified them to start drawing on Social Security.

The Baby Boom generation, those who were born between 1946 and 1964, has been responsible for changing nearly every industry that they've moved through – starting with baby food and schools. Today, Baby Boomers are moving swiftly in to other territory, namely health care and retirement income.

With roughly 10,000 Boomers turning 65 each and every day, this is putting an enormous strain on programs like Social Security and Medicare. Take, for instance, the Social Security system. This pay-as-you-go program uses money that is taxed on current workers to pay benefits for current retirees.

Back in 1935, when Social Security began, this seemed like a workable concept. Then, there were plenty of workers who were paying into the system, which made it much easier to fund benefits for the recipients.

Based on data from the Social Security Administration, back in 1940, there were roughly 222,000 Social Security benefit recipients and nearly 35.4 million workers who were paying into the system to fund their benefits. This equates to a ratio of nearly 160 workers for each Social Security benefit recipient.[3]

But my how times have changed. As the huge Baby Boomer generation has entered into their retirement years, the ratio of workers to Social Security recipients has been steadily declining - which in turn, has made funding these benefits much more difficult.

In 2008, when the first of the Boomers started turning age 62 (the age at which you can begin to take your Social Security retirement benefits), the ratio of workers to recipients had dropped all the way down to 3.2. And, in 2011, when the first Boomers began to turn age 65, the ratio dropped again to 2.9.[4]

Ratio of Social Security Covered Workers to Beneficiaries

Year	Workers	Recipients	Ratio
1940	35,390,000	222,000	159.4
1950	48,280,000	2,930,000	16.5
2008	162,485,000	50,420,000	3.2

2011	158,988,000	54,816,000	2.9
2013	163,221,000	57,471,000	2.8
2018	187,600,000 (est)	67,000,000 (est)	2.8

Source: Social Security Administration

By the year 2037, the Social Security Administration expects that the Social Security trust fund reserves will become exhausted. In other words, the switch will be flipped, and the more than $2.8 trillion in "spare" cash will start to dwindle.

How old will you be in 2037?

If you're planning to be retired, you'll likely be forced to rely less on Social Security and more on an income plan that you create. In addition to that, given the massive shortfall that is continuing to get worse, where do you think the money will come from when the Social Security Trust Fund runs out of cash to pay benefits?

If you guessed from taxes, you would be right!

In fact, the U.S. government will soon need large cash infusions to meet its commitments – and in turn, it will have no choice but to raise taxes.

But these taxes won't just come from the people who are still in the workforce. They will also be siphoned from retirees who are generating income from investments, pensions, and yes, even from their own Social Security benefits!

On top of that, the scales are tipped in the government's favor even more, because if (or in this case, when) it needs more money, it can increase the percentage of taxes it takes from you!

Unfortunately, these taxes – coupled with lower Social Security retirement income benefits - can make a tremendous difference in how, and how well, you - and your loved ones - will live in the future.

So, ask yourself whether your retirement would be better if you were able to spend only 50% (or less) of the income you're generating, or 100%. I'm pretty sure I know what your answer would be.

You Can Run From Uncle Sam's Taxes, But You Cannot Hide

On top of simply getting his hands on some (or most) of your money, Uncle Sam will also give you a deadline for when you have to start giving it to him if you have been investing in a traditional IRA and / or other type of qualified retirement plan like a 401(k).

For the most part, these plans allow you to take a deduction on the money you contribute. This can be a nice perk - at least in the short-term - as these pre-tax contributions allow you to forgo paying income tax on the amount that you put in.

Your funds in these accounts are also allowed to grow tax-deferred. That means you don't need to worry about paying tax on the gain in the account - at least not quite yet. But, as we will discuss in more detail later on in this book, deferring your tax obligation does not mean that it will go away.

In fact, deferring your tax obligation can actually make things worse - much worse - for you down the road, especially if your account balance has grown.

Being no dummy, Uncle Sam knew exactly what he was doing when he came up with these rules. That's because, his portion of the tax - at the time you withdraw your money - is likely to be far more than what it would have been if it was based solely on the amount of your contribution.

So, when you really think about it, the more your accounts grow over time, the more tax you'll have to pay, since 100% of your withdrawal from traditional IRAs and qualified accounts is typically subject to taxation.

Plus, if you take "early withdrawals" from these types of accounts (i.e., before you turn age 59 1/2), the government will charge you an additional 10% "early withdrawal" penalty.

Required Minimum Distributions Equate to Required Taxation

Given this sad but true information, you may be asking, what if you don't need the money in your traditional IRA or other retirement account(s), and you opt to just leave it in your account to continue accumulating over time?

Sorry. No go.

That's because your traditional retirement accounts are also subject to Required Minimum Distributions (or RMDs).

Based on the provisions in the SECURE (Setting Every Community Up for Retirement Enhancement) Act, which took effect on January 1, 2020, Uncle Sam requires you to take at least a minimum amount out of traditional IRAs and employer-sponsored retirement plans when you turn age 72.

Prior to 2020, required minimum distributions were to begin at age 70 ½. At that time, investors were also no longer allowed to make additional contributions into these plans. Starting in 2020, the maximum age for traditional IRA contributions has been eliminated.

But even though you can keep contributing to these accounts, the end result could actually cause you to pay even more taxes on your distributions. The amount you are required to withdraw is "conveniently" determined by an IRS-created formula. And when you withdraw this minimum amount - even though you may or may not really need it - Uncle Sam gets even more of his share of the pie.

It also reduces the balance in your account - which could turn out to be a tremendous detriment to how long your portfolio can sustain you over time. And if you run out of money, then what?

The Government's Piece of the Pie is Getting Bigger

With thousands of Baby Boomers retiring every day, Uncle Sam is usually the biggest beneficiary of the money that was saved by individuals. And, just as the stock market is unpredictable, no one knows what tax rates will be in the future.

So, just as you're getting ready to settle down in retirement, you'll more than likely have a nice big tax bill due - and Uncle Sam will collect, regardless of whether your portfolio is up or down.

Accumulation is often the name of the game for most financial advisors. But, as funds grow inside of traditional IRAs, 401(k)s, and other tax-deferred savings plans, the government is also keeping a close eye on "their" money.

While you may not currently be paying taxes on the gains in your qualified plans, it is important to keep in mind that in most cases, the taxes in these plans are just simply being deferred, but they are certainly not being eliminated.[5]

In other words, Uncle Sam isn't saying that you won't owe the tax. He's simply saying that you can pay it later...and later usually means that your tax liability will far exceed the deduction that you received on the contribution.

For many people, the taxes that are owed on these types of withdrawals can be even more than the total amount contributed - although there is no guarantee that the market will be up when you are ready to start taking your withdrawals.

So, the real question is, are you saving and investing to enhance your retirement lifestyle, or are you gambling with your current and future wealth?

Good Savers and Investors are Penalized the Worst

The tax system in the United States has become so confusing and convoluted that, even if you've been a good saver and investor all of your life, you won't get to keep very much of the "spoils," In fact, in many cases, the more you make, the more Uncle Sam will get - that is, unless you have some good planning strategies in place.

Unfortunately, what most people have been taught as the "traditional" methods of planning for future income and asset transfer has been extremely misleading - that is, of course, unless you want to hand over a substantial amount in taxes to the government.

So really, the only way to protect yourself from the impact of rising taxes is to adopt a strategy that puts you in the 0% tax bracket in retirement. That what my company specializes in.

Using our exclusive STEP (Strategic Tax-free Evaluation Process), our clients are able to reclaim what is rightfully theirs, and reduce – or even eliminate altogether – the amount that goes to Uncle Sam.

Chapter 2 Key Takeaways

- A major financial storm is on the way – and not planning for it could cost you
- Roughly 10,000 Baby Boomers turn age 65 every day
- There is tremendous strain on Social Security and Medicare
- The top Federal income tax rate has been as high as 90%...and it could be again
- You may be in a HIGHER tax bracket in retirement
- You are required to withdraw money from certain accounts at age 72

Chapter 2 Action Steps

- Determine how much of your retirement income will come from taxable accounts

Chapter 2 Questions to Consider

1. True or False: Most retirees are in a lower tax bracket than they were during their working lives.

2. True or False: Setting money aside in a traditional IRA or 401(k) can actually end up doing you more harm than good.

3. True or False: In the future, tax rates are likely to keep going down.

4. The U.S. government will soon need large cash infusions to meet its commitments, and in turn, it will have no choice but to _____.
   a. Lower taxes
   b. Raise taxes
   c. Increase Social Security benefits
   d. Increase Medicare benefits

5. The funds in a traditional IRA and 401(k) are allowed to grow _____.
   a. Tax free
   b. Tax deferred
   c. Indefinitely
   d. None of the Above

Chapter 2 Answers

1. False. It is quite possible that you could be in the same – or even in a higher – tax bracket in retirement, depending on how much income you have.

2. True. Even though you may be able to deduct your contributions into a traditional IRA and 401(k) – and your earnings can grow tax-deferred – when the time comes to make withdrawals, Uncle Sam will be able to tax you on a much larger piece of the "pie."

3. False. While we don't know what the income tax rates will be years down the road, we do know that they are much more likely to go up than they are to go down.

4. The U.S. government will soon need large cash infusions to meet its commitments – and in turn, it will have no choice but to raise taxes.

5. The funds in a traditional IRA and 401(k) are allowed to grow tax deferred – meaning that taxes will be due at the time of withdrawal. The problem is, we don't know what tax rates will be in the future.

Chapter 2 Sources

1. U.S. Debt Clock. https://usdebtclock.org/ Accessed December 26, 2019.
2. Ibid.
3. Social Security History. https://www.ssa.gov/history/ratios.html
4. Ibid.
5. The Baker's Secret to Permanent Family Wealth. By John Cummuta.

Chapter 3: Retirement Plan Tax Magic

Who is Really Benefitting from Your Life Savings?

"We contend that for a nation to try to tax itself into prosperity is like a man standing in a bucket and trying to lift himself up by the handle." -- Winston Churchill

Given all of the trouble that's been brewing in the U.S. retirement system over the years, many people today will need to supplement their Social Security and / or their pension (if they even get a pension at all) with income that is generated from personal savings and investments.

According to data from the U.S. Bureau of Labor Statistics from 2018, only about 55% of the adult population participates in a workplace retirement plan – and of those, many are far behind when it comes to investing a portion of their paycheck.

For instance, Vanguard reports that in early 2019, the median 401(k) balance for those who were age 65 and over was just over $58,000. That's not nearly enough to last even for a year or so, much less until age 80 or beyond. And with people living longer lives these days, it's not out of the question for someone to live for another 20 or more years after retiring.

This is where the SECURE Act comes in.

The Setting Every Community Up for Retirement Enhancement (SECURE) Act was approved by the U.S. Senate and signed into law in mid-December 2019, and became effective on January 1, 2020.

One of the key goals of this legislation was to increase access to tax-advantaged retirement savings and essentially help to prevent older Americans from outliving their assets.

Yet, even though the SECURE Act did provide some incentives for individuals and businesses, we all know that when Uncle Sam giveth, he also taketh away! And the SECURE Act is no exception.

SECURE Act Benefits to Individuals

One of the biggest incentives for individuals is that the SECURE Act pushes back the age at which required minimum distributions, or RMDs, must come out of traditional IRAs and retirement plans.

For years, investors who turned age 70 ½ have been required to start taking out at least a minimum amount (which is determined by life expectancy and an IRS formula for withdrawals) from such plans.

If they do not, they are penalized, based on the amount that should have come out of the plan. At that same time, investors were to cease making any additional contributions into these traditional plans.

The SECURE Act has now bumped that required minimum distribution age back from 70 ½ to 72, which gives investors roughly 18 additional months to receive tax-deferred growth on the funds that are inside of these accounts.

They can also forgo paying taxes for an additional year and a half on the money that is withdrawn – which is typically 100% taxable. In addition, investors are no longer required to stop making contributions into these plans at any age.

The SECURE Act added a couple of other benefits for individual investors, too, including:

- Penalty free withdrawals of $5,000 from 401(k) accounts to help with defraying the costs of either having or adopting a child;
- Allowing the use of tax-advantaged 529 college savings accounts for repayments of qualified student loans (up to a limit of $10,000 per year);
- Taxpayers who have high medical bills may also be able to deduct unreimbursed expenses that exceed 7.5% (in 2019 and 2020) of their adjusted gross income. In addition, individuals may withdraw money from their qualified retirement plans and IRA accounts penalty-free in order to cover expenses that exceed this threshold (although it is important to note that regular taxes will apply, and that the threshold returns to 10%, from 7.5%, in the year 2021).

Benefits to Small Businesses and Employees via the SECURE Act

If you're a business owner or you're employed by a small business, the SECURE Act can have some benefits here, too. For instance, this legislation will make it easier for small business owners to set up "safe harbor" retirement plans that are less expensive and easier to administer.

In addition to that, many part-time workers will now be eligible to participate in employer retirement plans under the bill. So, even if you work fewer than 40 hours, you could still be allowed to save and invest in a tax-advantaged manner through your workplace.

In this case, part-time employees who work either 1,000 hours through the year, or who have three consecutive years with 500 hours of service, are allowed to sign up for the employer-sponsored savings plan.

Workers will also begin to receive annual statements from their employers estimating how much their retirement plan assets are worth, expressed as a monthly income received over a lifetime. This should help workers to better gauge progress towards meeting their retirement income goals.

The SECURE Act also encourages retirement plan sponsors to include annuities as an option in workplace plans by reducing their liability if the issuing insurance company is not able to meet its financial obligations.

Because annuities are virtually the only financial vehicle that can guarantee the payment of a lifetime income – regardless of what happens in the market, or how long the recipient needs it – this can be a definite plus for employee/investors.

Where Uncle Sam Makes the Tradeoff

As nice as it may seem for the government to "help" investors with saving for the future, there is usually a "tradeoff" – and the passage of the SECURE Act is no exception – starting with the elimination of the "stretch IRA."

In many cases, individuals who are not an investor's spouse will inherit IRA (Individual Retirement Account) funds from a decedent. If this is the case with you, it is important that you have a plan in place to protect as much as possible from being taxed so that your beneficiary can make use of the money, rather than simply handing a large chunk of it over to Uncle Sam.

For instance, while life insurance proceeds are typically free of income taxation for the beneficiary, other assets – such as the proceeds from an IRA – may not be. In this case, a "stretch" IRA strategy was frequently used in the past to help ease the burden of excessive taxation all at one time by "stretching out" the inherited IRA distributions throughout the beneficiary's lifetime.

Using a stretch IRA also allowed for continued tax-deferred growth for the funds that were still in the account. So, even though the beneficiary's distributions would eventually be taxed, the tax deferral provided the opportunity to grow and compound the funds inside of the IRA.

But based on the SECURE Act, which took effect on January 1, 2020, this is no longer the case. By eliminating the stretch IRA, non-spousal IRA beneficiaries are now required to withdraw all of the funds in an inherited IRA within ten years after the death of the original account holder – regardless of the age of the beneficiary. (These rules also apply to inherited 401(k) accounts, regardless of whether they are rolled into a traditional or a Roth IRA).

This means that the entire balance of the account must be distributed after the tenth year. Although there are no requirements that the beneficiary take out a minimum amount of funds each year (as there is with the RMD rules), all of the money must be out of the account at the end of the ten-year time period.

Limiting the time that a beneficiary has to take distributions can potentially increase the tax burden on the recipient. These new rules can be particularly problematic for beneficiaries who are in their 40s and 50s, and who are generally at the peak of their earning years (and in turn, in a higher income tax bracket). This, in turn, can be highly beneficial for Uncle Sam.

In fact, according to the Congressional Research Service, the elimination of the stretch IRA has the potential to generate more than $15 billion in tax revenue to the government over the next decade. With that in mind, it could make a lot of sense to consider converting some or all or a traditional IRA to a Roth, which can be inherited income tax free.

Although the Roth IRA conversion would be taxable at the time it occurs, investors who spread out a series of conversions over the next several years may benefit from the lower income tax rates that are set to expire in 2026.

Another alternative for helping to reduce the amount that comes out of an IRA beneficiary's pocket when inheriting an account would be to have the account holder purchase a life insurance policy (using some or all of the funds from the required minimum distribution). Then, when the account holder passes away, the death benefit from the policy could be used by the plan beneficiary for paying the taxes that are owed on the withdrawal(s).

To make this strategy even sweeter, the earlier a life insurance policy is purchased, the lower the premium is likely to be for an ample amount of coverage. For instance, by looking at the charts below, you can see – based on the age, gender, and smoking/non-smoking class of the insured / IRA account holder – just how much protection could be purchased.

Life Insurance Coverage for Females

Age	Class	Initial Death Benefit	Initial Annual Premium
60	Non-Smoker	$518,088	$10,000

62	Non-Smoker	$463,863	$10,000
65	Non-Smoker	$393,370	$10,000
67	Non-Smoker	$347,607	$10,000
70	Non-Smoker	$291,019	$10,000

(Note that these quotes can differ from one individual to another, as well as from one insurance company to another. These particular quotes are based on females who are residents of the state of Illinois).

Life Insurance Coverage for Males

Age	Class	Initial Death Benefit	Initial Annual Premium
60	Non-Smoker	$435,728	$10,000
62	Non-Smoker	$389,553	$10,000
65	Non-Smoker	$330,533	$10,000
67	Non-Smoker	$295,878	$10,000
70	Non-Smoker	$251,586	$10,000

(Note that these quotes can differ from one individual to another, as well as from one insurance company to another. These particular quotes are based on males who are residents of the state of Illinois).

While some of the solutions for reducing or eliminating taxes might initially seem overwhelming, going over all of your specific short- and long-term goals and objectives with a financial professional – and particularly one who is well versed in retirement income and tax strategies - can point you in the right direction.

The good news here is that a qualified STEP advisor can offer suggestions on how to reduce the amount of tax a beneficiary is subject to – even if they are required to withdraw a substantial amount of money over a short period of time.

Chapter 3 Key Takeaways

- Only about 55% of the adult population in the U.S. participates in a workplace retirement plan.
- The median 401(k) balance in 2019 was just over $58,000.
- One of the primary goals of the SECURE Act was to increase access to tax-advantaged retirement savings and help prevent older Americans from outliving their assets.
- The SECURE Act pushes back the age at which required minimum distributions must begin, from 70 ½ to 72.
- Contributions to traditional IRAs and retirement plans no longer have to stop at any age.
- 529 college savings accounts may be used for student loan repayments.
- Taxpayers may be able to use qualified retirement plan assets for paying medical expenses.
- Part-time workers may now be able to participate in employer-sponsored retirement plans.
- Retirement plan sponsors can now include annuities as an option in workplace retirement plans.
- Non-spouse beneficiaries who inherit qualified funds must access the entire balance of those funds within 10 years (and thus pay the required taxes).

Chapter 3 Action Steps

- Determine how much more you could contribute to – and earn in - a traditional retirement plan between age 70 ½ and 72.
- If your traditional IRA and/or employer sponsored retirement plan beneficiary is not your spouse, make sure that you have a plan for reducing, paying, or even eliminating the taxes that will be due.

Chapter 3 Questions to Consider

1. True or False: All IRA account holders must stop making contributions at age 72, based on the provisions of the SECURE Act.
2. Required minimum distributions from a traditional IRA account must begin at age _____.
   a. 70
   b. 70 ½
   c. 72
   d. Never
3. True or False: One of the key goals of the SECURE Act was to increase access to tax-advantaged retirement savings and help prevent older Americans from outliving their assets.
4. True or False: Based on the SECURE Act, employers are no longer allowed to include annuities as an option in workplace plans.
5. Non-spouse IRA beneficiaries have _____ years to access the entire account that they have inherited.
   a. 1
   b. 5
   c. 10
   d. Unlimited time

Chapter 3 Answers

1. False. Required minimum distributions from a traditional IRA and/or retirement plan must begin at age 72. There is no age limit now, based on the SECURE Act, for ceasing IRA contributions.
2. Required minimum distributions from a traditional IRA account must begin at age 72.
3. True.
4. False. The SECURE Act encourages retirement plan sponsors to include annuities as an option in workplace plans by reducing their liability if the issuing insurance company is not able to meet its financial obligations.
5. Non-spouse beneficiaries have 10 years to access the entire account that they have inherited.

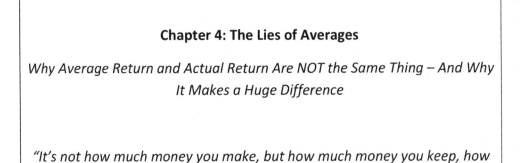

Chapter 4: The Lies of Averages

Why Average Return and Actual Return Are NOT the Same Thing – And Why It Makes a Huge Difference

"It's not how much money you make, but how much money you keep, how hard it works for you, and how many generations you keep it for." -- Robert Kiyosaki

Have you ever invested money that gave you disappointing results, even though the "average return" over time showed a positive figure?

If so, you're not alone – and unfortunately, the "average return" spiel is something that's been used by financial advisors for many years. In a lot of cases, though, even the advisor doesn't realize what a racket this really is.

But I'm going to show you right now.

The Illusion of Average versus Actual Returns

Most stock market benchmarks, such as the Dow Jones Industrial Average, as well as most mutual funds, will provide their average returns over a certain period of time. Typically, these time periods are short, such as one year, as well as long, such as five, ten, twenty, or more years.

These average returns are touted all over the place, and – provided that they are positive, they are usually presented to prospective investors (of course, with the caveat of "past returns are not indicative of future performance").

But even if the investment has a stellar performance in a given year, the actual dollar amount that you are positive or negative won't necessarily reflect a substantial gain. That is because, the more your return falls in one year, the more it will have to make up going forward just to get you back to even again.

Notice the chart below. If, for instance, your investment drops by 20% in Year1, it will need to go back up by 25% just to get back to square one. If it drops by 50% in Year 1, a 100% gain is required the following year just for it to get back to even, and so on.

Percent Loss Drawdown vs. Percent to Recover	
% Loss of Capital	% of Gain Required to Recoup Loss
10%	11.11%
20%	25%
30%	42.85%
40%	66.66%
50%	100%
60%	150%
70%	233%
80%	400%
90%	900%
100%	broke

In looking at actual dollar figures, let's say that you invested $10,000 into an account, and in the first year, the return drops 50%. In this case, you would end up with $5,000 at the end of Year 1.

In Year 2, the account experiences a positive 50% gain. So, are you back to having the original $10,000 you started with?

Nope!

Not even close – because a 50% gain on $5,000 will bring you to $7,500, not $10,000. Therefore, your account balance at the end of Year 2 is still 25% less than the $10,000 you started with at the beginning of Year 1.

Let's take this example one step further. In Year 1 you had a return of -50%, and in Year 2 you experienced a return of 50%. That comes to an average return of 0% - right?

Yes, that part is true. Your AVERAGE return is 0%. But, because you started out with $10,000 and you now have only $7,500 your ACTUAL return is negative 25%.

In fact, as long as there are any negative numbers in the mix, the actual return will never equal the average return. Here is an example of how a $1,000 investment that vacillated between positive and negative yearly returns of 10% would look over a ten-year period of time.

End of Year	Gain or Loss	Value of Account
1	10%	$1,000.00
2	(-10%)	$990.00
3	10%	$1,089.00
4	(-10%)	$980.10
5	10%	$1,078.11
6	(-10%)	$970.30

7	10%	$1,067.33
8	(-10%)	$960.60
9	10%	$1,056.66
10	(-10%)	$950.99

Source: The Retirement Miracle. By Patrick Kelly.

Here again, even though the average return is zero, the actual return is roughly a negative 5%. With that in mind, be careful of the "smoke in mirrors" tactic used by investment advisors who try to lure you in with "average" returns – because oftentimes, the returns they are showing you are nowhere close to the actual performance.

What if there was a way that you could attain an actual return of more than 60% with the exact same zig-zagging 10% ups and downs?

Stick with me, and I'll show you how!

Chapter 4 Key Takeaways

- Average return is not the same as actual return.
- Even if your investment has a stellar performance in a given year, the actual dollar amount that you are positive or negative won't necessarily reflect a substantial gain.
- The more your return falls in one year, the more it will have to make up going forward just to get you back to even again.

Chapter 4 Action Steps

- Determine what the ACTUAL return on your money is – and then compare it to the stated average return. These will likely be very different numbers!

Chapter 4 Questions to Consider

1. True or False: Average return and actual return are the same thing.

2. If an investment drops by 50% in a given year, a gain of _____ is required the following year just for it to get back to even.
   a. 20%
   b. 25%
   c. 50%
   d. 100%

3. True or False: If your average return is 0%, your actual return can still be in the negative.

4. True or False: The more an investment's return falls in one year, the more it will have to make up going forward just to get back to even again.

5. True or False: As long as there are any negative numbers in an investment's returns, the actual return will never equal the average return.

Chapter 4 Answers

1. False. Average returns and actual returns can differ significantly.

2. If an investment drops by 50% in a given year, a gain of 100% is required the following year just for it to get back to even.

3. True. If you had a return of -50% in Year 1, and a return of 50% in Year 2, your average return is 0%, but your actual return is actually -25%.

4. True.

5. True.

Chapter 5: The Definition of Retirement Insanity

Doing What We've Always Done and Expecting a Different (and Better) Result

"All taxes discourage something. Why not discourage bad things like pollution rather than good things like working or investment." -- Lawrence Summers

Are you using the most tax-efficient methods when it comes to saving, investing, and taking distributions (or future distributions) from your financial accounts?

You may *think* that you are.

But if you follow most of the "traditional" financial rules - which consist in large part of growing your retirement savings tax-deferred - then you may have a big surprise coming later on when you must hand over what could be a sizeable portion of your retirement income in taxes.

As we will discuss in much more detail later in this book, tax-deferred means exactly what it says - *deferred*, but not eliminated. In fact, by deferring your tax liability now, it is very likely that you will be required to pay more tax in the future...and believe me, Uncle Sam is well aware of that.

Whose Rules are You Playing By?

Today's financial "rules" allow the government to be much more in control of your assets than you'd probably like them to be. Take, for example, the traditional IRA or 401(k) plans. It's possible that you've spent most of your working life contributing to these types of investment vehicles. But, if you're under age 59 1/2, you'll be penalized by the IRS for taking an "early withdrawal" if you want or need your money.

This penalty is in addition to the income taxes that you'll pay. Those taxes, by the way, will typically be levied on the entire amount that you withdraw, since you were given a tax deduction when you initially contributed the funds.

You could wait until you are over the age of 59 1/2 to start taking your money out. But, if the funds in your retirement plan have grown at all, Uncle Sam will still be the recipient of a nice sized income tax bill - one that is likely many times more than the income tax deduction that you received years ago on the contribution. With that in mind, you're being taxed on the entire amount of your mature **"crops"**, when you only received a tax benefit on the much smaller **"seed"**.

During the dozen years between age 59 1/2 and age 72 (the age when required minimum distributions must begin from traditional retirement accounts), the income tax may be the "only" thing you owe to Uncle Sam when you take withdrawals from your retirement savings (as you'll no longer be hit with the 10% penalty). But, if you haven't started making your withdrawals by the latter age, you could be faced with penalties once again - this time, for not taking your Required Minimum Distribution.

That Required Minimum Distribution penalty is 50% of the amount that you were required to take out of the account. Why are you required to start taking withdrawals at that time? Well, because Uncle Sam wants his money! And the amount that you will owe him in retirement is unknown – and completely out of your control.

A Look Back at Taxes in the U.S.

Federal (and state, where applicable) income tax rates have varied widely for more than 100 years in the United States, with the highest federal rate hitting 94% in 1944 and 1945 - and with a number of other years also seeing the top rate in excess of 90%.

In 2018, after a massive tax reform, the top marginal income tax rate of 37% hits taxpayers who have taxable income of $500,000 or more for single filers, and $600,000 and higher for married couples who file jointly. As you can see from the chart below, though, rates have moved around quite a bit throughout the last century in the United States.

Top Federal Income Tax Rates 1913 – 2020

Year	Rate	Year	Rate
2018-2020	37	1950	84.36
2013-2017	39.6	1948-1949	82.13
2003-2012	35	1946-1947	86.45
2002	38.6	1944-1945	94
2001	39.1	1942-1943	88
1993-2000	39.6	1941	81
1991-1992	31	1940	81.1
1988-1990	28	1936-1939	79
1987	38.5	1932-1935	63
1982-1986	50	1930-1931	25
1981	69.125	1929	24
1971-1980	70	1925-1928	25
1970	71.75	1924	46
1969	77	1923	43.5
1968	75.25	1922	58
1965-1967	70	1919-1921	73
1964	77	1918	77
1954-1963	91	1917	67
1952-1953	92	1916	15
1951	91	1913-1915	7

Source: Inside Gov (http://federal-tax-rates.insidegov.com/)

So, relying on income that may or may not be what is projected - coupled with an unknown income tax rate in the future - is kind of a silly way to plan for the rest of your life. And, this shaky planning can become even more faulty if you run into unexpected expenses along the way.

For instance, what if you have a pricy health care need?

Long-term care can be expensive - nearly $100,000 per year in some areas of the U.S. Even with Medicare - which, by the way, pays very little for long-term care services - it is estimated that the average couple who retired in 2019 at age 65 will need roughly $285,000 to cover medical expenses in retirement.[1]

Even if you've been saving diligently over the years, it's likely that your advisor has touted the benefits of growing your money tax-deferred. Admittedly, not having to pay tax in the current year on your investment gains can be nice.

But just simply putting off your taxes until a later date doesn't mean that they're going to go away. In fact, if you're lucky enough to have nice gains in your tax-deferred accounts like a traditional IRA or 401(k), your tax obligation is actually getting bigger with each passing day.

Tax-Deferred Does Not Mean Tax-Free

Although they may sound similar, tax-deferred and tax-free are two entirely different concepts. For example, an account that is tax-deferred will eventually have taxes due on the funds that come out of it, whereas with a tax-free account, you can withdraw money without taxes being levied.

There are a number of different types of investment accounts that qualify either as tax-deferred or tax-free - and it is important that you know how your money is being treated with regard to the taxes in each.

Tax-Deferred	Tax-Free
Traditional IRA	Roth IRA
SEP IRA	Roth 401(k)
SIMPLE IRA	Roth 403(b)
401(k)	Roth 457
Profit Sharing	529 Plan
403(b)	Coverdell Education Savings Account
457 Plan	Health Savings Account (HSA)
Qualified Annuity	Life Insurance Policy Loans
Non-Qualified Annuity	

One of the best examples between tax-deferred and tax-free is with the Traditional and Roth IRA accounts. In this case, a Roth IRA offers tax-free accumulation. Contributions are made into a Roth IRA with money that has already been taxed.

So, the gains that are attained by those contributions will be tax-free, provided that the account has been open for at least five years, and the account holder is at least age 59 1/2 or older. Being able to withdraw funds tax-free can equate to much more net income, which in turn can be used for paying more of your everyday expenses and / or for other things like travel and fun.

On the other hand, Traditional IRA accounts (as well as most 401k and other traditional employer-sponsored retirement plans today) allow investors to take a deduction on some - or even all - of their contributions. This means that the amount of the contribution won't be included on that year's income tax return, and therefore won't be subject to income taxation at that time.

While the money that is accumulated inside of these Traditional accounts will also be allowed to grow and compound without yearly taxation, when these funds are withdrawn, they are oftentimes fully taxable at your then-current income tax rate. (And even though many financial advisors tout that you will likely be in a lower tax bracket in retirement, this is not necessarily the case).

Plus, if you make withdrawals from these types of plans before you turn age 59 1/2 (unless you meet one of the very few exceptions that are allowed by the IRS), you will also owe the IRS an additional 10% "early withdrawal" penalty. (This penalty is in addition to the taxes you'll owe). So, depending on your tax bracket, this could mean that you'll be handing over roughly half of the amount of your withdrawal to Uncle Sam.

How Much of Your Income Will Uncle Sam Take From You?

Whether you're working full time, you're the owner of a business, or you are a full-fledged retiree, it is likely that you receive income from somewhere - and in many cases, you might even receive income from several different sources, such as wages, interest, dividends, royalties, rent, and / or commissions.

In many cases, the money that you earn is likely going to be taxable - at least to some extent. This is particularly the case if you are still actively working. But, what you do with your money after it's been earned can make a world of difference in your lifetime, as can the way in which taxes are (or are not) applied to an investment - particularly over a long period of time.

Based on the manner in which you file your taxes - single, married filing jointly, married filing separately, or head of household - you can fall into one of many different tax brackets. In 2020, these brackets, along with the associated income tax rates, are noted below:

Tax Brackets and Rates (2020)

Rate	Single Individuals, Taxable Income Over:	Married Filing Jointly, Taxable Income Over:	Head of Household, Taxable Income Over:
10%	$0	$0	$0
12%	$9,875	$19,750	$14,100
22%	$40,125	$80,250	$53,700
24%	$85,525	$171,050	$85,500
32%	$163,300	$326,600	$163,300
35%	$207,350	$414,700	$207,350
37%	$518,400	$622,050	$518,400

Source: Internal Revenue Service

So, as an example of how your income tax is determined, let's say that you are single, and you earn just $100 more than $9,875 in 2020, for a total of $9,975. In this case, you would owe 10% tax on the money that falls into the first bracket - which is 10% on the first $9,875 that you earned.

But then you would also owe 12% on that additional $100 that spilled over into the next tax bracket. So, that additional $100 would be taxed at a higher rate than the first $9,875 that you earned.

In total, then, your income tax would be calculated as follows:

$9,875 X 10% = $987.50

+

$100 X 12% = $12.00

Total Tax Due = $999.50

Although that may not seem like a large amount of tax, what if you made ten times that amount...or twenty times...or more. As your income, and in turn, your income tax rate goes up, so does the percentage of money that you hand over to Uncle Sam. And the more you give to him, the less you have to put into your own pocket.

But does this mean that everyone who makes more money will have to pay a higher percentage of income tax?

Not necessarily. And especially not if you're using the STEP plan to reduce or eliminate tax and keep more of your money for yourself.

In fact, the man who many people tout as the greatest investor in the world, Warren Buffett, has stated that his secretary pays a higher percentage of income tax than he does.

How is this so? There are actually a couple parameters that come into play here.

First, his secretary is not married, so she files her tax return as a single individual. And second, her taxable income is $60,000. By using the figures in the table above, Mr. Buffett's secretary will pay 10% on the first $9,875 she earns. This equates to $987.50.

She will then owe 12% on the amount of income she earns between $9,875 and $40,125. This means that the next $30,250 ($40,125 - $9,875 = $30,250) garners a tax of $3,630 ($30,250 X 12%).

And, the amount of money she earns between $40,125 and $60,000 will have an income tax of 22%. So, in terms of dollar figures, this component of her income, which is $19,875 ($60,000 - $40,125 = $19,875), will be responsible for $4,372.50 in tax, for a total income tax of $8,990. All told, then, the secretary pays roughly 15% in income tax.

Now, it's highly likely that Warren Buffett brings in a lot more than $60,000 in income per year - and that he pays out more than $8,990 in income tax. So, what exactly does he mean when he says that his secretary pays a higher percentage of income tax than he does?

Well, while the dollar figure of his income likely has more zeros, because Warren Buffett earns most of his income through capital gains as versus wages, the percent of tax that is owed is smaller.[2]

This is because capital gains are not taxed according to the regular income tax schedule. Rather, capital gains have their own tax rates, which for long term capital gains, is either 0%, 15%, or 20% (in 2020). This applies to assets that were held for more than a year.

Short term capital gains tax rates on most assets that are held for less than one year correspond to ordinary income tax rates, which for 2020 are 10%, 12%, 22%, 24%, 32%, 35%, or 37%.

In addition to the lower tax brackets for long-term capital gains, there are also various other "loopholes" that can allow people to keep more of their own money. In fact, there are strategies that can take you all the way down to paying 0% on your income.

One way is to take advantage of the Roth IRA. The other, believe it or not, is through a properly orchestrated life insurance policy. These types of plans allow you to STEP around the income tax that most other retirees will be required to pay.

What exactly does that mean for you? For one thing, it means that you'll have more spendable income in the future that can be used for items that you need and want – and quite frankly, it can make your retirement a whole lot more enjoyable...and less worrisome.

And the earlier you put these plans in place, the more time you'll have for them to provide you with these benefits, and the less you'll be handing over to Uncle Sam. At FRA Trust, we help our clients do this every day. We'll also be discussing this in the next chapter.

Chapter 5 Key Takeaways

- Investing the way "it has always been done" isn't the way to attain the best results.
- Today's financial "rules" allow the government to be much more in control of your assets than you'd probably like them to be.
- You can incur taxes and / or penalties on your retirement funds.
- Tax-deferred is not the same as tax-free.
- Oftentimes, investors are taxed on the entire amount of their mature "crops" (i.e., the growth on their money), when you only receive a tax benefit (deferral) on the much smaller "seed."

Chapter 5 Action Steps

- Ask yourself, "Whose rules are you playing by?" Then determine where you can reduce, or even eliminate, the tax liability on your hard-earned money.

Chapter 5 Questions to Consider

1. True or False: Tax deferred and tax free mean the exact same thing.

2. By deferring your tax liability now, it is likely that you will have to pay _____ tax in the future.
   a. More
   b. Less
   c. The same

3. Which of the following allow you to take tax-free withdrawals?
   a. Roth IRA
   b. Roth 401(k)
   c. Life Insurance loans
   d. All of the Above

4. If you make a withdrawal from your traditional IRA plan before you turn _____, you will incur an "early withdrawal" penalty.
   a. 72
   b. 70 ½
   c. 50
   d. 59 ½

5. In 2020, the highest federal income tax rate is _____%.
   a. 22
   b. 32
   c. 35
   d. 37

Chapter 5 Answers

1. False. Tax deferred means that taxes are deferred until a later time – but they are not eliminated.

2. By deferring your tax liability now, it is likely that you will have to pay more tax in the future.

3. There are a number of accounts that allow you to take tax-free distributions, including Roth IRAs, Roth 401(k)s, Roth 403(b)s, Roth 457s, 529 Plans, Coverdell Education Savings Accounts, Health Savings Accounts, and life insurance policy loans.

4. If you make withdrawals from traditional IRAs (as well as most other types of qualified plans) before you turn 59 1/2, you will incur a 10% early withdrawal penalty from the IRS.

5. In 2020, the highest federal income tax rate is 37%.

Chapter 5 Sources

1. Health Care Price Check: A Couple Retiring Today Needs $285,000 as Medical Expenses in Retirement Remain Relatively Steady. Fidelity. https://www.fidelity.com/bin-public/060_www_fidelity_com/documents/press-release/healthcare-price-check-040219.pdf
2. Young Savers Rule(s): Tax-Free Snowball Magic. By Tom Guignon & Meade Greenberg.

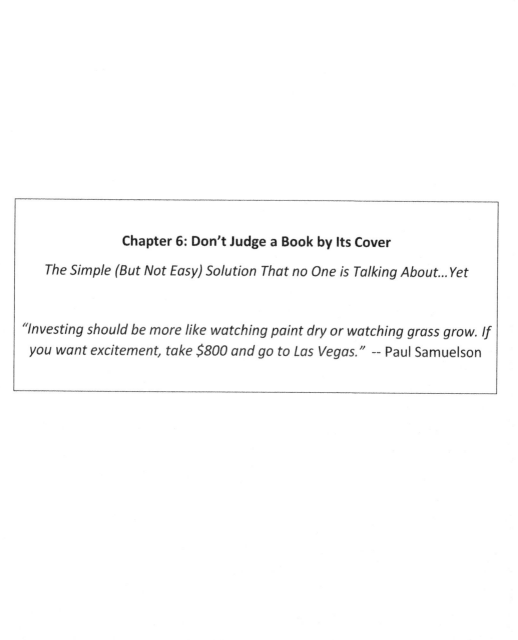

Chapter 6: Don't Judge a Book by Its Cover

The Simple (But Not Easy) Solution That no One is Talking About...Yet

"Investing should be more like watching paint dry or watching grass grow. If you want excitement, take $800 and go to Las Vegas." -- Paul Samuelson

With all of the rules and regulations in place as it pertains to retirement income, it can be difficult to really do what you want to do with your own money. But what if I told you there was a way that you could eliminate having to pay nearly half of your distribution to Uncle Sam and instead receive distributions tax-free?

Would you be interested?

Hopefully, you are - because there are ways to do just that (and yes, they are legal!), and with just a bit of planning, you could enjoy much more money in your own pocket - and that of your loved ones - as versus that of the tax man.

Tax Benefits of the Roth IRA

One way to ensure that you will have tax-free income in retirement is to open a Roth IRA. You may be familiar with the term IRA, which stands for Individual Retirement Account. By definition, an IRA is a retirement investment account established by employed workers who earn a salary, wage, or self-employment income.

Deposits for traditional IRAs are tax deductible and the investment earnings in the account are not taxable until withdrawn. In addition to the tax benefits received with IRA accounts, there are other benefits that make them attractive, too.

For example, retirement plans are generally given special protections from creditors, making them very useful for asset protection purposes. In addition, when structured properly, IRA assets can even be passed on to heirs for many generations to come.

Individual Retirement Accounts were initially established in 1974. Since then, they have grown in popularity as a way for investors to deposit and grow additional retirement funds (aside from an employer-sponsored plan like a 401k).

Provided the you meet certain guidelines, a Traditional IRA allows you to deduct your contributions in the tax year they are made, while investment earnings can accumulate tax deferred.

Upon reaching retirement age, or at least age 59 ½, traditional IRA distributions are treated as ordinary income. When you reach age 72, you are required to start taking at least a minimum amount of distributions from your traditional IRA.

Roth IRAs were implemented in 1998 as a result of the Taxpayer Relief Act of 1997. The money contributed to a Roth IRA is not deductible from ordinary income. So, you aren't allowed to make pre-tax Roth contributions. But if you meet certain income requirements, all earnings with be tax-free when you withdraw them at a later date, and your gains will never be taxed. And this can be an extremely worthwhile tradeoff!

In addition, there are no mandatory withdrawal requirements with a Roth IRA at any age, so you may leave your funds in the account to continue growing tax-free indefinitely.

Unfortunately, there are certain limitations on who is allowed to contribute to a Roth IRA. For example, (in 2020) if you file your taxes as a single individual, and you earn $124,000 or more in income, you may not be able to make a full contribution - which is $6,000 per year if you're age 49 and under, or $7,000 if you are age 50 or over. And, if your income exceeds $139,000 (in 2020), you are not eligible at all for this type of account.

Likewise, if you are married and you file your taxes jointly, you may make a reduced Roth IRA contribution if your modified adjusted gross income is between $196,000 and $206,000 (in 2020). But if your income exceeds $206,000 you may not make a contribution to a Roth IRA.

But even so, that doesn't mean that you have to forgo the opportunity for tax-advantaged growth – or even the receipt of tax-free income down the road. On top of that, you may also be able to create a pool of cash, tax-free, that can be used for critical, chronic, or terminal illness expenses, as well as a whole host of other needs, both now and in the future. On top of all *that*, you may even be able to put this strategy into effect at no out-of-pocket cost to you!

It's important to remember that the purpose of a retirement account is not to give you a tax deduction, it is to maximize your retirement distributions at a point in your life when you can least afford to pay the taxes – in retirement.[1]

The Roth IRA is one of the few accounts available today that is allowed to provide tax-free income. So, it is absolutely essential that you take advantage of a Roth – especially as income tax rates are much more likely to go up than they are to go down any time soon.

If you earn "too much" income to contribute to a Roth IRA, there may still be a way for you to participate in this type of account. For instance, a "backdoor" Roth IRA is a legal strategy for getting around the IRS income limits that typically restrict higher income earners from contributing to Roths. We will discuss this strategy in more detail in Chapter 8.

Exploring the Life Insurance Retirement Plan

You might be surprised to learn that one of the other ways to receive tax-free income in retirement is by setting up a certain type of life insurance plan. But, contrary to popular belief, life insurance can provide much more than just death benefit proceeds when an insured passes away.

In addition, going this route to obtain a good, solid return, along with a whole host of other benefits is not a new concept. In fact, far from it. There is a long list of wealthy individuals and business owners who have used the power of life insurance to start and grow their companies, and to ensure that they left a long-lasting legacy.

Just some of these include:

- James Cash "JC" Penney
- Walt Disney
- Ray Kroc

Likewise, life insurance encompasses one of the largest assets on the balance sheets of large and powerful financial institutions, such as Wells Fargo, Bank of America, JPMorgan Chase Bank, and U.S. Bank.[2]

No, life insurance may not sound nearly as exciting as stock options, commodities, or various other investments that are discussed at cocktail parties – as well as by the "gurus" on TV. But the long list of benefits that it can provide for you and those you care about is nothing short of astonishing...starting with its many tax advantages.

In the words of David McKnight, author of The Power of Zero, "You don't have to love life insurance or even life insurance companies, you just have to like them a little bit more than you like the IRS. Because in the end, not utilizing a life insurance retirement plan may actually keep you out of the 0% tax bracket, in which case, the IRS wins."[3]

Using a properly structured permanent life insurance policy allows you to build up cash value on a tax-deferred basis, while at the same time ensuring that if the unexpected occurs, your loved ones will receive a lump sum of money, free of income taxation.

Depending on which type of permanent life insurance policy you choose, you could reap some added benefits, too. For example, an indexed universal life insurance policy has a cash value component that earns its return primarily based on the returns of an underlying market index (such as the S&P 500). This gives you the opportunity to obtain market-linked returns – usually up to a specified cap.

However – and this makes the indexed universal life insurance policy even more advantageous – if the underlying market index has a down year, your funds don't lose value. In fact, the worst that you can do is 0%.

So, if you recall from our earlier example that showed actual return versus average return, a period of negative performance can hinder upward performance – and depending on how badly an investment performs in a given period of time, it could even require future return to be double that in order to just get you back to even.

That being said, take a look at what happens when you take the same $1,000 from that previous example, and put it into an indexed universal life insurance policy. Let's say that the underlying index performs in an identical fashion, being up 10% one year, and down 10% the next, for each of the following ten years.

Unlike a regular investment, though, with an indexed universal life insurance policy, your cash value would be credited with a 0% every other year, instead of incurring a 10% loss. At the end of the previous taxable example, the value of the investment was approximately 5% below the initial investment. ($950.99 at the end of Year 10).

Here's how the cash in the indexed universal life plan would perform:

End of Year	Gain or Loss	Value of Account
1	10%	$1.000.00
2	0%	$1,100.00
3	10%	$1,210.00
4	0%	$1,210.00
5	10%	$1,331.00
6	0%	$1,331.00
7	10%	$1,464.10
8	0%	$1,464.10
9	10%	$1,610.51
10	0%	$1,610.51

Source: The Retirement Miracle. By Patrick Kelly.

As you can see, even in the very same market conditions, the taxable account and the indexed universal life cash value attained very different results.

Plus, in addition to the protection of principal that the indexed policy offers, it also brings to the table a feature known as an annual reset. This essentially allows you to capture and lock in each year of positive return.

Therefore, even in a negative market, there is no need to climb out of the negative return hole in order to get back to square one. All of the gains that you get are yours to keep – no matter what happens in the market in the future - thus allowing you to continue building on them.

But the advantages of using life insurance for retirement planning don't stop there - especially when compared to many of the "traditional" savings and investment products that investors have been using for years.

For instance, some of the other key benefits that can be attained by using life insurance in retirement planning include:

- **No income limit.** Unlike a Roth IRA account, there is no income limit for participants, meaning that those who are higher income earners can still have the opportunity to use this type of planning.
- **No age limit.** A life insurance retirement plan will also not penalize you for taking distributions prior to age 59 ½. (There may, however, be surrender, or early withdrawal, charges. But I'm going to show you how you can get around that later in the book).
- **No contribution limit.** Also unlike IRAs and qualified retirement accounts, there is no limit on how much you can contribute to a life insurance policy each year. So, even if you have "maxed out" these other plans, you can still contribute to your life insurance policy - with no upper limit.
- **No Required Minimum Distribution requirements.** Unlike the traditional IRA and 401(k) – which now require that you start taking distributions from the plan at age 72 - there is no such rule with life insurance. So, if you don't need the money, it can remain in the policy's cash value and continue to grow on a tax-advantaged basis.
- **Protection from creditors.** In many instances, the money in your life insurance policy is protected from creditors. So, even in the event of a lawsuit or other situation that could threaten your personal assets, these funds will typically be safe.
- **The plan is self-completing.** Because of the death benefit that is associated with life insurance policies, the plan is considered to be "self-completing." This means

that, even in the event of the unexpected, survivors will still be protected financially with the policy's income-tax free death benefit.

If you've heard or read negative things about life insurance - which you probably have - I ask that you just simply lay those things aside for now as you learn more about what this truly amazing financial vehicle can do.

Using Life Insurance to Secure Your Tax-Free Retirement

Market volatility, coupled with longer life spans, the uncertainty of Social Security, and constantly rising inflation, means that investors need to supplement income sources - and adding life insurance to your retirement plan could offer an ideal solution.

In fact, the benefits that can be attained in a properly structured cash value life insurance policy are a prime example of strategically evaluating your future tax situation, and then implementing a viable solution.

Let's take a look at an example of how using life insurance to supplement retirement income could work - along with all of the other benefits it offers. In this hypothetical example, John, a 38-year-old male, opts to contribute $2,000 per month into his policy for a total of 15 years. This equates to a total contribution for John of $360,000 over that time.

Plus, because John is contributing these funds into a life insurance policy, he also is covered by a death benefit - in this case, the benefit is $640,000, and it would be paid out to his beneficiary, income tax free, if something were to happen to John.

As time goes on, due to the tax-deferred nature of the cash value in John's policy, the funds really start to compound. That is because John's money is earning interest on the principal, as well as interest on the interest, and interest on the money that would have otherwise been paid out in taxes. This, in turn, has a type of snowball effect.

When John turns 65, he starts taking distributions from the policy in the amount of $81,922 per year. He takes these distributions for 26 years, which amounts to more than $2.1 million in total distributions (even though he only paid in $360,000 of premium). And, if John passes away at age 90, his survivors / beneficiary would still receive a death benefit of nearly $346,000.

Here is a snapshot of John's contributions, as well as his distributions over time:

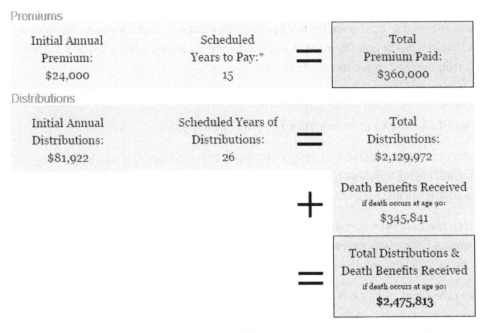

Premiums

| Initial Annual Premium: $24,000 | Scheduled Years to Pay:* 15 | = | Total Premium Paid: $360,000 |

Distributions

| Initial Annual Distributions: $81,922 | Scheduled Years of Distributions: 26 | = | Total Distributions: $2,129,972 |

+ Death Benefits Received
if death occurs at age 90:
$345,841

− Total Distributions &
Death Benefits Received
if death occurs at age 90:
$2,475,813

Source: Local Life Agents

Tax-free distributions can make a tremendous difference in how much you have available to spend on the goods and services that you need going forward. But you can't just implement this strategy with any given life insurance policy. Rather, the policy must be structured properly, and ideally by an insurance professional who specializes in life insurance retirement plans.

Take a look at an example here of a universal (permanent) life insurance policy that I purchased at age 53. This is actually just one of six life insurance policies that I own – and all are performing in a similar fashion.

On the far left of the illustration, you can see the amount of premium I put in, as well as when I plan to stop funding the plan. Also take a look at the cash surrender value column, and how it continues to grow, even though I had started to take distributions from the policy (shown under the Planned Annual Income column).

*Current Basis A Values — Illustrated Variable Loan Rate: 4.00%   *Current Basis B Values — Illustrated Variable Loan Rate: 4.00%

Policy Year	Planned Premium	Planned Annual Income	Weighted Average Interest Rate	Accumulated Value End Year	Cash Surrender Value End Year	Death Benefit End Year	Planned Annual Income	Weighted Average Interest Rate	Accumulated Value End Year	Cash Surrender Value End Year	Death Benefit End Year
5	$ 73,315	$ 0	4.00%	$ 362,105	$ 328,706	$1,789,995	$ 0	7.14%	$ 371,372	$ 337,973	$ 1,799,263
6	79,980	0	3.97%	439,384	411,126	1,867,275	0	7.01%	461,259	433,001	1,889,150
7	79,980	0	3.97%	518,986	496,026	1,945,877	0	7.03%	556,699	533,738	1,984,590
8	79,980	0	3.98%	600,995	583,504	2,028,886	0	7.04%	658,067	640,576	2,085,958
9	79,980	0	3.98%	685,379	673,513	2,113,270	0	7.05%	765,641	753,775	2,193,532
10	79,980	0	3.98%	772,105	766,065	2,199,995	0	7.05%	879,715	873,675	2,307,606
11	79,980	0	3.99%	874,838	874,838	2,302,729	0	7.10%	1,015,706	1,015,706	2,443,597
12	79,980	0	3.99%	980,852	980,852	2,408,742	0	7.10%	1,160,647	1,160,647	2,588,538
13	79,980	0	3.99%	1,090,289	1,090,289	2,518,179	0	7.10%	1,315,212	1,315,212	2,743,103
14	79,980	0	3.99%	1,203,300	1,203,300	2,631,190	0	7.10%	1,480,123	1,480,123	2,908,014
	$ 793,135	$ 0					$ 0				
15	79,980	0	3.99%	1,320,040	1,320,040	2,747,930	0	7.10%	1,656,157	1,656,157	3,084,048
16	79,980	0	3.99%	1,440,741	1,440,741	2,868,632	0	7.10%	1,844,222	1,844,222	3,272,113
17	79,980	0	3.99%	1,566,083	1,566,083	2,868,632	0	7.10%	2,046,080	2,046,080	3,272,113
18	0	256,641	3.99%	1,619,627	1,352,721	2,601,725	256,641	7.11%	2,185,556	1,918,649	3,005,207
19	0	256,641	3.99%	1,674,848	1,130,358	2,324,142	256,641	7.11%	2,336,109	1,791,620	2,727,624
20	0	256,641	3.99%	1,731,841	898,666	2,035,456	256,641	7.11%	2,498,964	1,665,789	2,438,937
21	0	256,641	3.99%	1,790,726	657,317	1,735,222	256,641	7.12%	2,675,542	1,542,133	2,138,704
22	0	256,641	3.99%	1,851,640	405,987	1,422,979	256,641	7.12%	2,867,496	1,421,844	1,826,461
23	0	256,641	3.99%	1,914,748	144,362	1,098,246	256,641	7.13%	3,076,759	1,306,374	1,501,728
24	0	0	0.00%	0	0	0	256,641	7.13%	3,304,314	1,196,207	1,361,423
	$1,033,075	$1,539,846					$ 1,796,487				
25	0	0	0.00%	0	0	0	256,641	7.13%	3,548,561	1,089,223	1,266,651
26	0	0	0.00%	0	0	0	256,641	7.13%	3,810,371	985,752	1,176,271
27	0	0	0.00%	0	0	0	256,641	7.13%	4,090,897	886,387	1,090,932
28	0	0	0.00%	0	0	0	256,641	7.13%	4,391,370	791,773	1,011,342
29	0	0	0.00%	0	0	0	256,641	7.13%	4,713,097	702,610	938,263

			*Current Basis A Values Illustrated Variable Loan Rate: 4.00%					*Current Basis B Values Illustrated Variable Loan Rate: 4.00%			
Policy Year	Planned Premium	Planned Annual Income	Weighted Average Interest Rate	Accumulated Value End Year	Cash Surrender Value End Year	Death Benefit End Year	Planned Annual Income	Weighted Average Interest Rate	Accumulated Value End Year	Cash Surrender Value End Year	Death Benefit End Year
30	$ 0	$ 0	0.00%	$ 0	$ 0	$ 0	$ 256,641	7.13%	$ 5,057,494	$ 619,680	$ 872,555
31	0	0	0.00%	0	0	0	256,641	7.13%	5,425,913	543,681	814,977
32	0	0	0.00%	0	0	0	256,641	7.13%	5,819,718	475,290	766,276
33	0	0	0.00%	0	0	0	256,641	7.12%	6,240,239	415,127	727,139
34	0	0	0.00%	0	0	0	256,641	7.12%	6,688,718	363,695	698,131
	$1,033,075	$1,539,846					$ 4,362,897				
35	0	0	0.00%	0	0	0	256,641	7.12%	7,166,608	321,677	680,007
36	0	0	0.00%	0	0	0	256,641	7.12%	7,675,403	289,768	673,538
37	0	0	0.00%	0	0	0	256,641	7.12%	8,216,803	268,836	679,676
38	0	0	0.00%	0	0	0	256,641	7.12%	8,792,492	259,699	699,324
39	0	0	0.00%	0	0	0	256,641	7.12%	9,413,645	272,634	649,180
40	0	0	0.00%	0	0	0	256,641	7.12%	10,086,004	312,447	615,027
41	0	0	0.00%	0	0	0	256,641	7.13%	10,815,359	383,953	600,260
42	0	0	0.00%	0	0	0	256,641	7.13%	11,611,694	496,125	612,242
43	0	0	0.00%	0	0	0	256,641	7.13%	12,464,420	637,321	761,966
44	0	0	0.00%	0	0	0	256,641	7.13%	13,377,513	810,423	944,198
	$1,033,075	$1,539,846					$ 6,929,307				
45	0	0	0.00%	0	0	0	256,641	7.13%	14,355,814	1,019,134	1,162,693
46	0	0	0.00%	0	0	0	256,641	7.13%	15,404,520	1,267,467	1,421,512
47	0	0	0.00%	0	0	0	256,641	7.13%	16,528,420	1,558,978	1,724,262
48	0	0	0.00%	0	0	0	256,641	7.13%	17,734,324	1,899,198	2,076,541
49	0	0	0.00%	0	0	0	256,641	7.13%	19,028,234	2,292,796	2,483,078
50	0	0	0.00%	0	0	0	256,641	7.13%	20,416,554	2,744,792	2,948,957
51	0	0	0.00%	0	0	0	256,641	7.13%	21,906,173	3,260,633	3,479,695
52	0	0	0.00%	0	0	0	256,641	7.13%	23,504,482	3,846,214	4,081,258
53	0	0	0.00%	0	0	0	256,641	7.13%	25,219,411	4,507,906	4,760,100
54	0	0	0.00%	0	0	0	256,641	7.13%	27,059,470	5,232,598	5,523,192

*Benefits and value are not guaranteed. The assumptions on which they are based are subject to change by the insurer. Actual results may be more or less favorable.

This illustration assumes payments are made in the amounts shown and that the illustrated rates and monthly deductions will continue in the future. The interest rate used in the calculation of current values is the weighted average rate shown in the columns below.

Similar to John's policy in the previous example, my plan continues to grow and compound each year. For instance, let's say that I beat the life expectancy odds and live to age 84. In this case, the numbers look quite good – which typically isn't the case for those who are relying on income from equity-related investments for a long period of time.

Premiums:

- Annual Premium: $79,980
- Years to Pay: 17
- Total Premium Paid: **$1,033,075**

Distributions:

- Initial Annual Distributions: $256,641
- Scheduled Years of Distributions: Life
- Total Distributions: $3,592,974
- Death Benefits Received: $814,555 (If death occurs at age 84)
- Total Distributions & Death Benefits Received: $4,407,529 (if death occurs at age 84)

Let's take it a step further and say I live to 100. Here again, the amount of annual premium and the total amount of premium paid in says the same, at 17 years and a total paid in of $1,033,075. But the difference comes in the amount of the distributions.

In this case, though, I can take annual distributions of $256,641 for a full 30 years, which gives me a total amount of distribution of a whopping $7,699,230. Plus, if death occurs at age 100, there will also be an income tax-free benefit for my survivors of $1,724,262.

*Disclaimer: The above is a hypothetical illustration. All situations and results can vary.

But the advantages of using life insurance for retirement planning don't stop there - especially when compared to many of the "traditional" savings and investment products that investors have been using for years.

There are some other key items to know before you put a life insurance retirement plans into motion. For instance, if you take a "traditional" distribution (a.k.a. a withdrawal from the policy's cash value), the money is considered to be ordinary income, which is taxable, just like it would be if you took it from a Traditional IRA or 401(k).

So, it takes proper planning and the right structure to keep all of your distributions tax-free – but it can be done!

Want to see how much you could generate in tax-free income, while at the same time ensuring that those you care about are covered "just in case?" Our STEP advisors can show you a customized illustration that is designed, based on your specific situation and goals.

How can you find a STEP trained advisor? Just visit: http://fratrust.com/next-step/ or call 618-632-8558 and request a STEP advisor directly.

You can also simply fill out a few details by emailing: marketing@fratrust.com for an evaluation form, and we'll make sure that you receive your free, no obligation hypothetical.

Let's take another look at income taxes, and how the brackets have most recently been revised. Here is how the Federal income tax brackets changed between 2017 and 2018 for single filers:

2017 Tax Rate	Single Filers	2018	Single Filers
10%	$0 - $9,325	10%	$0 - $9,525
15%	$9,326 - $37,950	12%	$9,526 - $38,700
25%	$37,951 - $91,900	22%	$38,701 - $82,500
28%	$91,901 - $191,650	24%	$82,501 - $157,500
33%	$191,651 - $416,700	32%	$157,501 - $200,000
35%	$416,701 - $418,400	35%	$200,001 - $500,000
39.6%	$418,401 or more	37%	$501,000 or more

And here's how it changed for married couples that file their taxes jointly:

2017 Tax Rate	Married Filing Jointly or Qualifying Widow / Widower	2018 Tax Rate	Married Filing Jointly or Qualifying Widow / Widower
10%	$0 - $18,650	10%	$0 - $19,050
15%	$18,651 - $75,900	12%	$19,051 - $77,400
25%	$75,901 - $153,100	22%	$77,401 - $165,000
28%	$153,001 - $233,350	24%	$165,001 - $315,000
33%	$233,351 - $416,700	32%	$315,001 - $400,000
35%	$416,701 - $470,000	35%	$400,001 - $600,000

39.6%	$470,001 or more	37%	$600,001 or more

Although the income amounts have changed, the income tax brackets remain the same, at 10%, 12%, 22%, 24%, 32%, 35% and 37% in 2020. But, taking a look at the difference in tax rates between 2017 and 2018, you can clearly see that the "cost" of getting to the 0% tax bracket just got a lot cheaper.

Unfortunately, this incentive is not slated to last forever. In fact, many of the 2018 tax incentives will "sunset", or expire, back to their old levels on December 31, 2025. So, if you really want to take advantage of them, doing so sooner rather than later can allow you more time to benefit.

The Way It's Always Been Done Isn't the Way It Always Should Be

As you can see from the examples above, by relying on money in a more "traditional" retirement plan, as well as from life insurance cash value withdrawals, you can plan on handing over a fairly large chunk of it to Uncle Sam.

But, if you take money out of a properly-structured life insurance policy by way of a policy loan, the distribution will be considered tax-free. This is because the IRS does not consider life insurance loans to be taxable income.

And, you can take it one step further, by having the money in your life insurance policy's cash value - even the amount that you've borrowed - continue to earn interest going forward.

How can this be possible?

The reason is because you are technically borrowing the money from the life insurance company itself, as versus directly from your own policy.

Imagine what your banker or stockbroker would say if you asked to take money out of your account to purchase a new vehicle or piece of real estate, while at the same time requesting that your money continue to earn interest, as if it was still there!

And the benefits with life insurance policy loans don't stop there. You could also have the opportunity to receive the money cost-free, as well as tax-free. This is because, even though the insurance company will charge you an interest rate on the borrowed funds, it could be offset by the interest that your money is continuing to earn.

As an example, if the insurance carrier charges you 2% (which is quite possible, as life insurance policy loans will oftentimes have a lower interest rate than traditional loans from banks and other lenders), and the money in your cash value is also earning a 2% rate of interest, then you have just secured a no-cost distribution.

It is important to keep in mind that, even though these types of loans are not required to be paid back, interest will still accrue. In addition, if you don't have at least some funds left in your policy's cash value when you (the insured) pass away, then the policy will lose its tax-free protection and as a result, all of the taxes that you were able to avoid will come due in that year.

It is also essential that you work with a STEP specialist to structure your policy loan provision just right. That is because, to many people, the difference between just 1% or 2% may seem insignificant when it comes to borrowing money.

But the reality is that it can make a tremendous difference in how much you can safely access from your policy each year, as well as how long you can continue to borrow before the plan essentially becomes "bankrupt."

So, it is incredibly important that you set up, and take distributions from, a plan that was created by someone who is well-versed in this specific area of life insurance planning. Otherwise, trying to do it yourself could end up costing you in the end.

Net Cost to Borrow

Age	Year	2% Spread Loan	1% Spread Loan	0% Spread Loan
65	1	$75,000	$75,000	$75,000
66	2	$75,000	$75,000	$75,000
67	3	$75,000	$75,000	$75,000
68	4	$75,000	$75,000	$75,000
69	5	$75,000	$75,000	$75,000

70	6	$75,000	$75,000	$75,000
71	7	$75,000	$75,000	$75,000
72	8	$75,000	$75,000	$75,000
73	9	$75,000	$75,000	$75,000
74	10	$75,000	$75,000	$75,000
75	11	$75,000	$75,000	$75,000
76	12	$75,000	$75,000	$75,000
77	13	$75,000	$75,000	$75,000
78	14	$75,000	$75,000	$75,000
79	15	$75,000	$75,000	$75,000
80	16	$75,000	$75,000	$75,000
81	17	$75,000	$75,000	$75,000
82	18	$75,000	$75,000	$75,000
83	19	$75,000	$75,000	$75,000
84	20		$75,000	$75,000
85	21		$75,000	$75,000
86	22		$75,000	$75,000
87	23		$75,000	$75,000
88	24			$75,000
89	25			$75,000
90	26			$75,000
91	27			$75,000
92	28			$75,000

93	29			$75,000
94	30			$75,000
Total Income:		$1,425,000	$1,725,000	$2,250,000
Total Cost:		$825,000	$525,000	$0

Analysis assumes a cash value of $1,000,000, an annual loan amount of $75,000 and a growth rate of 7.5%.

Source: Look Before You LIRP. By David McKnight.

By accessing tax-free loans from your life insurance retirement plan, there is another great benefit that you gain. These funds will not negatively affect the taxation of your Social Security income.

In other words, while there are numerous sources of provisional income that the IRS counts towards the earnings limit to determine whether or not – or how much – your Social Security benefits will be taxed, the money that you borrow from a life insurance retirement plan will not be included in this calculation.

In fact, income that comes out of a cash value life insurance policy – regardless of whether it is a withdrawal or a loan – will not subject your Social Security income to taxation. This, in turn, can allow you to keep more money in your pocket...and out of Uncle Sam's.

Calculating Your Own Tax-Free Benefits

A tax-free income advisor can help you in determining the type of benefit that you may attain if you go the route of our STEP process. In the meantime, though, you can also go to our tax-free income calculator and plug in the figures and information that is specific to you.

This calculator can be accessed by going to: http://faturl.com/frainfoandcalculator/?selected=0.

Pulling Millions of Dollars Out of Thin Air

On top of some pretty amazing cash value strategies, life insurance can also be used to pull additional dollars literally "out of thin air." For instance, in some cases, existing life insurance policies can be optimized to net the greatest return with the least cost.

Here, as an example, you could use cash value from an older life insurance policy and use it to purchase additional new insurance. In doing so, the cash value from the older policy can cover the difference between the amount that is needed and the amount that the current policy will return, at no additional cost to you.

Let's take the example of a man who has a $100 million estate, and needs $55 million for estate tax and other final expenses. He purchased a life insurance policy on himself several years ago - with an annual premium of $190,000 - that would allow his heirs to receive $8.7 million upon his passing.

By changing his coverage to a new second-to-die policy, which insures both he and his wife, he will end up receiving a much greater return. In this case, the same $190,000 per year will now purchase $29 million in life insurance coverage. With that in mind, his heirs will receive $20 million more - for the very same premium cost. This represents an increase in return of more than 300%.[9]

$20 Million at No Cost Example

Antiquated Policy

$190,000 Annual Premium
$8.7 Million Death Benefit

Transfer Cash Value to a New Second-to-Die Life Insurance Policy

New Second-to-Die Policy

Same $190,000 Annual Premium
$29 Million Death Benefit

Source: Die Rich and Tax Free. By Barry Kaye. Copyright 1997.

Doubling the Duties of Your Life Insurance Retirement Plan

In addition to all of the benefits of using life insurance as a retirement income tool, the advantages that can be gleaned from this financial vehicle don't stop there. Over the past several years, life insurance policies have morphed into instruments that can provide you with even more ways to protect you and your loved ones from financial devastation.

For instance, one area that could render you helpless (literally) is to have a long-term disability or an expensive long-term care need. Nobody likes to think that they'll end up in a nursing home someday - and thankfully, in most cases, people can get the care they need in the comfort of their very own homes.

But even that can cost you several thousand dollars per month - or more. So, depending on what you need, and how long you need it, this is an area that must absolutely be planned for in advance.

Otherwise, you could find yourself or your loved ones having to drain savings accounts (that are earmarked for other things) or needing to sell off investments or other assets (usually at a "fire sale" discount) in order to come up with the needed funds.

Even if you are able to spend what you need on long-term care, every dollar that goes to a facility or a caregiver is money that won't be available to your spouse and / or other loved ones for their own needs.

You may recall the statistic that was cited earlier - the one about a 65-year-old couple today needing to spend, on average, $280,000 out of their own pocket on health care costs throughout their retirement years.[4] You may also recall that figure did not include the cost of a long-term care need.

If you go with just the averages for long-term care expense, though, you could be looking at yet another 6-figure expense just for that. This can have the effect of drastically reducing your assets and income.

Historically, there have been a couple of strategies used for safeguarding against this type of expense. These include:

- Self-insuring
- Relying on family members as care givers
- Purchasing long-term care insurance

Unfortunately, none of these are really all that appealing. For instance, long-term care insurance is very expensive - and over time, as more insurance carriers have started paying out claims, the insurance companies backing these policies have been forced to raise their premium rates, or even to drop out of the business altogether. (Definitely one drawback to people living longer these days).

And then there's the question of, "What if I don't ever use it?" Here, although I've never spoken to anyone who was sad that they didn't use their long-term care insurance, years and years of paying premiums could end up to be an expensive gamble.

Self-insuring can also be costly, though, as it requires that you start out with a large sum of money, and then you hope that it lasts as long as you need it to. Unfortunately, as much as family and other loved ones mean well when (or if) they offer to become a caregiver, this too can be costly in terms of finances, as well as the physical, mental, and emotional toll it can take on a family.

The good news is that you have some other options here, too - and they could even come without you having to fork over a large premium each year for a stand-alone long-term care policy that you may or may not ever use. Yet, you could still receive monthly long-term care benefits.

Sound intriguing?

It should - and it can be easy to set up if you are already using life insurance as part of your retirement plan. In this case, there are life insurance policies available that will pay out a certain percentage of the death benefit if you qualify for a long-term care need.

So, as an example, if the policy pays 2% of the death benefit per month for long-term care, and the death benefit is $250,000, then you'd get a check, each and every month (until the end of the stated time frame) for $5,000.

But if you don't ever need long-term care, all is not lost. That's because the full amount of the death benefit would be paid out to your beneficiary (or beneficiaries) upon your passing - and they would receive these benefits tax-free.

Real Life Examples

Just like with any other type of financial product or service, not all plans are designed to work for every individual or families. But in the right scenario, the benefits can be very impressive. Here's how we were able to help one of our clients, Mary, and her daughter.

At the time we met with Mary, she was very ill, having already been diagnosed with cancer. Her doctor informed her that she only had a few months to live. So, Mary wanted to get her affairs in order.

Mary had $350,000 in her 401(k). The way it was positioned was that, if she left it to her daughter as is, more than one-third of the money could be lost to taxes. After reviewing her situation, we were able to help Mary with properly positioning her 401(k) and, upon her passing, Mary's daughter was able to receive the entire $350,000 instead of $227,500.

In addition to that, Mary's daughter was able to "stretch" that money so that it would last throughout her lifetime, which will provide her with nearly $2.6 million of financial security over time.

We were also able to help another client of ours, Ralph, with essentially "multiplying" his IRA. When we met with Ralph, he was 70 years old, and he owned a "passive" IRA. (This means that the money in his IRA, worth $1,000,000, was not money that he needed to live on).

Because of the Required Minimum Distribution rules, Ralph was required to take a distribution from his IRA in the amount of roughly $36,000 per year - and from that, pay more than $8,600 in taxes.

In addition, if he were to die and his IRA is inherited, it bears a tax titled "Income in Respect of Decedent." With this, the recipient would have had to pay taxes at their tax rate - which could also be bumped up to a higher bracket due to income.

We suggested that Ralph cash in his IRA. And, while he then owed a tax of $370,000 (ouch!), the remaining $630,000 bought a life insurance policy that had a death benefit of $3.25 million. Plus, because the life insurance policy was owned by a trust, the money is not only guaranteed to go to his heirs, but it was also able to pass both income and estate tax free.

If this planning had not been done and Ralph had kept his IRA as is, the recipient(s) would only have netted about $630,000. But now they are set to inherit roughly five times that amount. This equates to an increase in value of more than $2.6 million by simply re-positioning an asset.

As you can see, there are better ways to ensure that your retirement income, as well as the assets you've earmarked for those you love, is received in a much more tax-efficient manner. But, the plans you create must be established properly. Otherwise, you run the risk of losing the tax-related benefits...or worse.

Rather, getting the right advice from the right – and experienced – tax, legal, and financial professionals is crucial, both in creating and maintaining your plan.

Chapter 6 Key Takeaways

- There are ways to eliminate having to pay nearly half of your distribution to Uncle Sam, and to instead receive distributions tax-free.
- Roth IRAs are funded with after-tax dollars, but distributions are received tax-free.
- There are some limits on who can have a Roth IRA, and on how much you can contribute
- The right life insurance plan can provide tax-advantaged growth, protection of principal, tax-free access to the cash value, and possibly other benefits like protection from health care and long-term care expenses

Chapter 6 Action Steps

- If you have not already done so, and you qualify, open a Roth IRA and contribute the maximum amount to it each year.
- Determine which life insurance retirement plan you qualify for by talking with a trained STEP advisor.

Chapter 6 Questions to Consider

1. One way to ensure that you will have tax free income in retirement is to
   _____.
   a. Open a traditional IRA
   b. Open a Roth IRA
   c. Steal it
   d. All of the Above

2. True or False: Deposits for traditional IRAs are tax deductible, and the investment earnings in the account are not taxable until withdrawn.

3. True or False: Like a traditional IRA, there are also mandatory withdrawal requirements for Roth IRAs.

4. For those who are age 50 and over, you may contribute $_____ into a traditional or Roth IRA (in 2020).
   a. 5,000
   b. 6,000
   c. 7,000
   d. 10,000

5. A(n) _____ earns it return in large part based on the returns of an underlying market index such as the S&P 500.
   a. Whole life insurance policy
   b. Indexed universal life insurance policy
   c. Term life insurance policy
   d. None of the Above

Chapter 6 Answers

1. One way to ensure that you will have tax free income in retirement is to open a Roth IRA.

2. True.

3. False. There are no mandatory withdrawal requirements with a Roth IRA at any age, so you may leave your funds in the account to continue growing tax free indefinitely.

4. If you are age 50 or older, you may contribute up to $7,000 into an IRA in 2020.

5. An indexed universal life insurance policy has a cash value component that earns its return primarily based on the returns of an underlying market index (such as the S&P 500). This gives you the opportunity to obtain market-linked returns – usually up to a specified cap.

Chapter 6 Sources

1. The Power of Zero. How to Get to the 0% Tax Bracket and Transform Your Retirement. By David McKnight.
2. Money. Wealth. Life Insurance. How the Wealthy Use Life Insurance as a Tax-Free Personal Bank to Supercharge Their Savings. By Jake Thompson.
3. The Power of Zero. How to Get to the 0% Tax Bracket and Transform Your Retirement. By David McKnight.
4. How to plan for rising health care costs. Fidelity. April 18, 2018. https://www.fidelity.com/viewpoints/personal-finance/plan-for-rising-health-care-costs

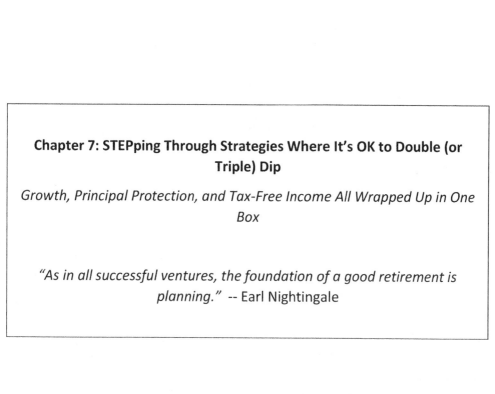

Chapter 7: STEPping Through Strategies Where It's OK to Double (or Triple) Dip

Growth, Principal Protection, and Tax-Free Income All Wrapped Up in One Box

"As in all successful ventures, the foundation of a good retirement is planning." -- Earl Nightingale

Obviously, a big part of attaining and maintaining wealth is investing wisely for retirement. Unfortunately, when it comes to doing that successfully, many people would likely agree that unknown – and volatile – marketing and economic conditions can present a great deal of challenges.

For example, if you are primarily seeking growth, you are oftentimes faced with having to take on too much risk in the hopes of achieving a higher return. And, if you are getting close to retirement, given your shorter time horizon, there is typically not enough time to recoup from loss to your portfolio.

On the other side of the coin, you could invest for safety and rid yourself of the worry about market volatility. But anyone who has checked the interest rates on bonds, CDs, and even fixed annuities lately is not likely jumping for joy at the 2% (or less) that is currently being offered.

So, how exactly do you go about finding a balanced approach to growing your money, while at the same time keeping it safe from a potentially downward moving market.

One option is to consider a fixed index annuity.

Considering a "Best of All Worlds" Financial Scenario

Keeping your money out of the reach of a downward moving market can provide a tremendous amount of value over time. One primary reason for this is because, if your account doesn't have to "come back" from negative years, it can continue to build on past years' growth.

Consider this. Regardless of how investors choose to invest their money for the future, there is typically one common theme among all – and that is those who are investing today's dollars into the market with a "buy and hold" strategy are betting their future income on the assumption that the market must regularly return to new highs. This can be especially detrimental when in the midst of a bear or downward moving market.

Yet, the question that investors must ask themselves is – what if the market doesn't return to previous highs?

And quite frankly, there is no guarantee that they will. Ever. And even worse yet, what if a bear market were to last for 10, 20, or even more years?

Will you be able (or even willing) to put off retiring for that much longer?

Probably not.

Unfortunately, in this case, the traditional buy and hold investment method (the method that countless investors go with, usually based on their broker's advice) would fail miserably – and there is no guarantee that the market will ever go up, down, or sideways at any given time.

A perfect example can be seen in what happened with the Nikkei 225, a Japanese stock market index that is connected to the third largest economy in the world, just behind the United States and China. This index can be considered as being similar to the U.S. S&P 500 index.

The Nikkei average hit an all-time high on back on December 29, 1989. This was during the peak of the Japanese asset price bubble when it reached in intra-day high of 38,957.44 before closing at 39,915.87.

Sadly, the Japanese investors who used the buy-and-hold strategy back in 1989 are still essentially "waiting" for the market to come back to its previous highs. In taking a look at the value of $1,000 invested in the Nikkei 225 from December 31, 1989 to December 31, 2009, investors can see that buying and holding is definitely not the way to go.

The value of $1,000 in the Nikkei 225 from 12/31/1989 to 12/31/2009

Year	End of Year Close	Annual Return	Value of $1,000
1989	38,915.90	NA	$1,000.00
1990	23,848.70	-38.72	$612.83
1991	22,983.80	-3.63	$590.60
1992	16,925.00	-26.36	$434.91
1993	17,417.20	2.91	$447.56
1994	19,723.10	13.24	$506.81
1995	19,868.20	0.74	$510.54
1996	19,361.30	-2.55	$497.52
1997	15,258.70	-21.19	$392.09

1998	13,842.17	-9.28	$355.69
1999	18,934.34	36.79	$486.55
2000	13,785.69	-27.19	$354.24
2001	10,542.60	-23.53	$270.91
2002	8,578.95	-18.63	$220.45
2003	10,676.60	24.45	$274.35
2004	11,488.76	7.61	$295.22
2005	16,111.43	40.24	$414.01
2006	17,225.83	6.92	$442.64
2007	15,307.78	-11.13	$393.36
2008	8,859.56	-42.12	$227.66
2009	10,546.44	19.04	$271.01

Source: The Retirement Miracle, by Patrick Kelly

While there were some positive years in this example, overall the market provided a negative return. In this case, even "waiting it out" for over 20 years returned the investor only $271 on a $1,000 investment.

That's nothing to brag about!

The truth is that those who employ the buy-and-hold strategy could even be subject to unlimited losses, as this technique calls for holding on to stocks – regardless of price signals or negative news regarding the market or the underlying company itself.

For instance, despite news and warnings that a company could be preparing to file bankruptcy or in the midst of a financial upheaval, buy-and-hold investors are still advised to "hang on" to their shares – even though at some point these shares may become completely worthless and cause the investor to lose his or her entire investment.

At times, investors may also become discouraged with their buy-and-hold strategy and will change course. This could be due to having a low risk tolerance during a market downturn or it may even be due to panic about losing funds.

This, too, however is not a good idea, as oftentimes there are fees involved for moving your invested funds. And, there is no guarantee that the new investment will perform any better than the old one did.

In fact, changing course mid-stream can be likened to a driver who changes lanes in a heavy traffic jam, only to discover that his new lane is now blocked while the lane he just moved out of is moving again!

What's Wrong with "Traditional" Retirement Planning – And What You Can Do About It

Many of today's investors – and especially those who are nearing retirement and / or have suffered significant market losses over the past few years – are now approaching the concept of saving for the future with a very different view than was taken just a mere decade ago.

Gone are the days when nearly any stock investment was practically guaranteed to provide investors a nice high return, and even the investment options that are considered to be "safer" such as bonds and CDs are not netting investors nearly what they will need in order to live a comfortable retirement lifestyle.

Yet, while a large part of investing has to do with the market – which essentially cannot be controlled – there are other factors that can be better planned for or at the very least avoided by investors so as to reduce or eliminate potential landmines to future wealth.

In fact, today we have more options available to us that can put investors firmly back into the driver's seat. One financial vehicle that is often considered to offer the best of all worlds is the fixed index annuity.

These financial vehicles offer their holders a unique combination of benefits that can provide tax deferred growth of funds within the account, along with the potential for a nice return based on indexed interest, and an amount of protection for the investor's retirement assets and income.

How and Why Fixed Index Annuities are Quickly Becoming the Option of Choice

The fixed index annuity can offer interest earnings potential that is linked to a market index, such as the S&P 500, yet it will completely avoid losses to its account during market downturns – regardless of how the underlying index performs.

This financial vehicle is very appealing to those who understand the long-term benefit of investing in equities but who are not comfortable with the volatility and potential losses that are a common part of investing in equities.

These products were created with the purpose of offering a return that is somewhere between stock market gains and basic savings instruments. With the typically higher returns than other conservative options, and coupled with the safety of principal that they can offer, fixed index annuities have become a very popular choice – especially for retirees and those who are approaching retirement.

So how exactly does a fixed index annuity work?

Like other types of annuities, fixed index annuities are insurance contracts between an investor and the offering insurance company. In exchange for a premium payment – either one lump sum or periodic contributions – the insurance company provides the investor with a stream of income in the future.

Also similar to other types of annuities, a fixed index annuity can be either immediate or deferred, meaning that benefits may be paid out to its holder either immediately (or very soon) after an initial lump sum deposit is made, or deposits can be made over time with benefits also being paid out over a series of years – or even for the remainder of the recipient's lifetime.

What makes these products different from regular fixed annuities is that the growth in the account is based on the performance of an underlying index – and the value of this index is tied to a stock market or other type of investment index. Some of the more common indices that are tracked by a fixed index annuity are the Standard & Poor's (S&P) 500 and the Dow Jones Industrial Average (DJIA).

These products are considered to be safer than variable types of products, however, because even though the fixed index annuity tracks a market index, the actual value of the annuity's account will not vary from day to day.

Rather, it is thought to be much more predictable in that the interest credited to the annuity is locked in on a regular basis – typically annually – on the annuity's anniversary date. Therefore, when the holders of a fixed index annuity purchase an annuity, they are still obtaining an insurance contract versus actually purchasing the shares in a stock or equity index.

Because fixed index annuities are technically an insurance contract, they can guarantee the safety of investors' principal as well as offer a minimum rate of return. This differs from variable annuity products in that these annuities offer the potential for high return, yet they do not protect the contract holder's principal should the underlying investments perform poorly.

In fact, a fixed index annuity can actually guarantee that the value of the account holder's investment will never be less than the sum total of their deposits while still offering the opportunity to exceed the fixed rate of return if growth in the underlying index exceeds the investor's minimum. Overall, a fixed index annuity can provide their holders with both security and stability.

Tracking the Life of a Fixed Index Annuity – And How You Can Benefit from Each

Fixed index annuities have two different phases. The first is what is referred to as the accumulation phase. This phase begins as soon as the investor starts making deposits into the annuity. During this time, the investor makes deposits into the account – or deposits one lump sum – and these funds will begin to earn interest within the account.

One big advantage is that the fixed index annuity account holder will receive at least a guaranteed amount of interest that is credited to the account. This interest is guaranteed by the insurance company or by an interest rate that is based upon the growth of an external index.

In addition, the investor will defer having to pay tax on this interest until they begin receiving their withdrawals – allowing the opportunity for these tax-deferred funds in the account to grow faster.

Typically, at the time that an investor purchases a fixed index annuity, they can decide upon which of the indexes (if there is more than one option available) the annuity's value will be allocated to.

In addition, the annuity holder is also able to choose which type of crediting method will be utilized in tracking the changes in their chosen index(es). There are different factors that are involved in tracking these changes.

These factors include:

- **Cap** – There are certain types of fixed index annuities that will set a maximum rate of interest – also referred to as a "cap" rate – that the annuity can earn within a certain period of time. Should the fixed index annuity holder choose an index that's increase is more than the cap amount, then the cap rate is used in determining the annuity holder's interest. The specified periods of interest calculation may be either monthly or annually.

- **Participation Rate** – The participation rate will determine how much of the underlying index's increase will be used in computing the indexed interest rate. For example, if a fixed index annuity holder's annuity uses a participation rate of 100 percent, then the annuity would receive 100 percent of the indexed interest that is achieved within a certain time period.

It is important to note that this calculation also assumes that there is not a cap or spread that applies, and that an annuity's participation rates are typically applied after the annuity's cap, yet before the spread.

- **Spread** – With some fixed index annuities, the indexed interest amount will be determined by subtracting a certain percentage from any gain that the underlying index achieves within a certain period of time. For instance, should the annuity have a spread of 4 percent and the index increases 9 percent, then the annuity will be credited with 5 percent indexed interest.

The accumulation phase is followed by the distribution phase. It is during this time that the investor receives an income stream from their funds in the annuity's account. This phase begins at the time that the account holder starts to receive their income payments.

The payments that are received by the investor may be in the form of a scheduled annuitization over a certain period of time – including an indefinite time period such as for the remainder of the account holder's life.

Many annuities also offer a death benefit option whereby a named individual or individuals may, depending on the situation, receive some or all of the deposited funds that have not yet been returned to the annuity holder should they pass away.

Another factor that FIA holders need to be aware of is the automatic annual reset. This factor is typically found in most fixed index annuity contracts. This feature allows the index values to automatically "reset" at the end of each contract year.

What this means is that the prior year's ending value will become the following year's beginning value in the annuity. In addition, the automatic annual reset feature will also lock in any interest that the fixed index annuity has earned during the year. Therefore, in essence, a negative index return from one year will not have an effect on the next year's potential for indexed interest.

Using an example, if an annuity is purchased that has an annual reset feature and the underlying market is down, then although no interest is credited to the fixed index annuity account, the annuity holder will also incur no losses and the annuity's value will automatically "reset" on its anniversary date at the same amount it was the prior year.

If, however, the underlying market has a positive return in a given year, the fixed index annuity will be credited with the gain and will thus reset on its anniversary date at the higher amount. This amount will then become the new base amount.

Overall, by having this feature, the FIA holder will earn no interest in down market years, but they will also not lose any value either. Therefore, the annual reset feature provides opportunity for higher return when the underlying index is up and protection when that index is down.

In addition, with annual reset on an FIA, the underlying index will not have to make up for previous losses in order for the annuity's account value to earn additional interest. This is because each contract year, the ending value of the annuity becomes the next year's beginning value.

The chart below highlights the annual reset feature on a fixed index annuity. It shows the actual S&P 500 historical data between January 1, 2000 and January 1, 2010.

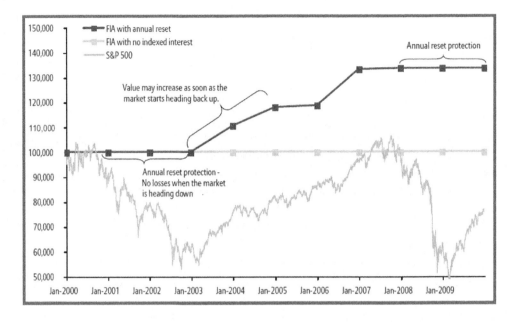

Source: "Fixed Index Annuities: What are the advantages of annual reset?" – Allianz Life

Providing an Income that Cannot Be Outlived – No Matter How Long

Similar to other types of annuities, a fixed index annuity allows its holder to convert the annuity's value into a series of income payments if they so choose. With this type of annuity, these income payments can be a fixed amount.

In addition to just the pure income benefits, however, fixed index annuities may also offer additional types of benefits or optional income riders that allow income payments to increase to help keep pace with inflation over time.

Fixed index annuity holders typically have two choices when it comes to receiving their annuity income. These include annuitization payments or income withdrawals. It is important to note that there are tax differences, depending upon which method the annuity holder chooses.

For example, if a fixed index annuity is not held within a qualified retirement account, such as a traditional IRA or 401(k), a part of each annuitization payment will be considered a tax-free return of what the annuity holder paid into the annuity and the other part is considered to be taxable as interest that was earned in the account.

So, it is important to note that the income withdrawals could be subject to the recipient's ordinary income tax rate. And, similar to many other types of retirement accounts, should the annuity holder withdraw funds prior to reaching at least age 59 ½, they may incur an IRS penalty of 10 percent for the early withdrawal.

There could, however, be a way for you to make the fixed index annuity even better by receiving tax-free income from it. How can you do that?

While many financial advisors tout on about how annuities shouldn't be placed in tax-advantaged accounts, I beg to differ. That's because having your fixed index annuity inside of a Roth IRA, you can take advantage of all of the benefits already included with this type of financial vehicle AND not have to pay a dime in income tax in the future when you're taking your income withdrawals.

How's that for a win-win-win-win scenario!

Creating a Comfortable Retirement While Leaving a Legacy for Future Generations

In addition to providing an income that cannot be outlived, fixed index annuities can also provide another attractive feature in that they can allow their holder to leave a legacy for his or her loved ones.

This allows the investor to make money available to a named beneficiary (or beneficiaries) in the event that the investor passes away and has not received some or all of the income from the annuity contract.

Oftentimes, the nominated beneficiary can decide whether they would like to receive the death benefit proceeds either in a single lump sum payment or via a series of regular payments received over time.

Is a Fixed Index Annuity Right for You?

Although the fixed index annuity might sound like the perfect way to keep money safe while at the same time having the opportunity to grow – and in the future, throwing off an income that lasts for your entire life – believe it or not, everyone is not an ideal candidate for this type of financial vehicle.

On top of that, with the myriad of annuity products that are available in the market place today, it is extremely easy to become overwhelmed. In fact, of all the types of annuities, fixed index annuities tend to have the most complex array of moving parts.

With that in mind, if you are leaning towards the purchase of a fixed index annuity, make sure that you have some guidance from a financial professional who understands how these products work, and how to determine which one may be best for you.

Chapter 7 Key Takeaways

- Investors must typically take on more risk if they want the opportunity for more reward, or alternatively, get miniscule returns with "safer" investment options.
- A fixed index annuity can offer interest earnings potential that is linked to a market index, such as the S&P 500, yet it will completely avoid losses to its account during market downturns – regardless of how the underlying index performs.
- Fixed index annuities can provide you with an income stream for the rest of your life – no matter how long that may be.
- You may be able to receive tax-free income from a fixed index annuity.

Chapter 7 Action Steps

- Discuss your short- and long-term financial objectives with an annuity specialist who can match you with the one that most closely fits your needs.

Chapter 7 Questions to Consider

1. "As in all successful ventures, the foundation of a good retirement is
   _____.
   a. Stocks
   b. Bonds
   c. Equities
   d. Planning

2. True or False: Those who employ the buy-and-hold investment strategy could be subject to unlimited losses.

3. True or False: The fixed index annuity can offer interest earnings potential that is linked to a market index, such as the S&P 500, yet it will completely avoid losses to its account during market downturns.

4. A fixed indexed annuity can provide you with which of the following.
   a. Safety
   b. Security
   c. Both A and B
   d. Neither A or B

5. True or False: One big advantage is that the fixed index annuity account holder will receive at least a guaranteed amount of interest that is credited to the account.

Chapter 7 Answers

1. According to Earl Nightingale, "As in all successful ventures, the foundation of a good retirement is planning."

2. False. Those who employ the buy-and-hold strategy could even be subject to unlimited losses, as this technique calls for holding on to stocks – regardless of price signals or negative news regarding the market or the underlying company itself.

3. True. The fixed index annuity can offer interest earnings potential that is linked to a market index, such as the S&P 500, yet it will completely avoid losses to its account during market downturns – regardless of how the underlying index performs.

4. A fixed index annuity can provide their holders with both security and stability.

5. True. One big advantage is that the fixed index annuity account holder will receive at least a guaranteed amount of interest that is credited to the account. This interest is guaranteed by the insurance company or by an interest rate that is based upon the growth of an external index.

Chapter 8: The Risk of Doing Absolutely Nothing

Deer in the Headlights Are Often Hit by Oncoming Cars!

"Do something today that your future self will thank you for." --
Anonymous

Enjoying a retirement that is free from taxes can take both strategic and proactive planning – and this planning must start right now, because the longer you wait, the less likely you are to reap the benefits.

How many times have you heard financial "gurus" in the media say things like, "Don't worry about future taxes. You'll be in a lower tax bracket when you retire."

Really? How so?

I challenge that thinking – and for a number of very good reasons.

First, you are likely to have far fewer tax deductions when you reach retirement. For instance, if you are withdrawing funds from your savings or investments – or even if you've just simply said goodbye to your employer – will you still be making tax-deductible (or any) contributions into your tax-qualified retirement account?

Probably not.

It's also much more probable that you'll have your home mortgage paid off when you're retired, which in turn means that you won't be deducting mortgage interest. This alone is one of the biggest tax deductions that most people have.

On top of that, as a retiree, your children will likely be long past the age where they can be considered a dependent. So here, too, you lose out on yet another tax deduction. (That's not to say that adult children won't move back into the proverbial "nest," though. They just can be taken as a tax deduction!)

During your working years, you may have contributed to a favorite charity. As a retiree, however, you might be able to offer more of your time, but you may not have a lot of extra funds to donate. So, this is yet another tax deduction that many people lose out on once they have reached retirement.

Even if you are still planning to work for several more years, you could lose out on some key deductions if you wait too long to take action. In the last few waning hours of 2017, President Donald Trump passed his long-promised tax reform in the United States. With this reform came a number of key changes, including:

- A reduction in the top Federal income tax rate from 39.6% to 37%
- Doubling of the standard deduction
- Elimination of personal exemptions
- Elimination or reduction of many itemized deductions, such as:
  - Deduction for property taxes and / or state / local income taxes limited to $10,000
  - Deduction for alimony

- ○ Mortgage / home equity interest deduction
- Elimination of the "Please Amendment" limitation on deductions, which means that those who do continue to itemize can do so without limits.

In addition, the estate tax exemption was increased to just under $11.2 million per taxpayer, with a 40% tax on transfers that exceed the amount of this exemption. Likewise, the gift, estate, and generation skipping tax exemptions increased, per individual, from $5 million to $10 million.

History of Estate Tax Exemptions

1980's - Estates Under $400K

1990's - Estates Under $600K

2000's - Estates Under $1.2M

2010 - Estates Under $2.5M

2013 - Estates Under $5.5M

2018 - Estates Under $11.18M

2019 – Estates Under $11.4M

2020 – Estates Under $11.58M

But, while some of these new tax changes may be beneficial, it is important to keep in mind that virtually all of these provisions are only temporary - and they are slated to sunset after the year 2025, reverting back to the previous level. Because of that, it is key that, if you want to take advantage of these tax breaks, it is essential that you do so now rather than later.

Earning Income in Retirement Can Backfire When It Comes to Taxes

If you're like many people, you may decide to work during retirement. Whether that entails taking on a part-time job, or even starting a new business that you've always wanted to try, unfortunately this could end up costing you.

That's because, if you start taking Social Security benefits before what is considered your "full retirement age," and you earn more than a stated amount of annual income, a portion of your Social Security benefits could be taxed.

The most common sources of provisional income include:

- Employment income
- Rental income
- Interest from municipal bonds
- Distributions taken from tax-deferred accounts (such as a 401k, traditional IRA, etc.)
- Interest and 1099 income generated from taxable investments
- One-half of your Social Security income

Once you start taking your benefits, the IRS will add up all of your provisional income for the year, and based on how your file your tax return, you could have up to 50% or 85% of your Social Security income taxed.

Here are the income limit figures (in 2018):

Joint Provisional Income for Married Couples

Provisional Income	% of Social Security Subject to Tax
Under $32,000	0%
$32,000 to $44,000	50%
Over $44,000	85%

Source: Social Security Administration

Individual Provisional Income for Single People

Provisional Income	% of Social Security Subject to Tax
Under $25,000	0%

$25,000 to $34,000	50%
Over $34,000	85%

Source: Social Security Administration

So, while you could do nothing and keep your retirement savings the way they are, you run the risk of Uncle Sam being the biggest beneficiary of your retirement income – and the amount that he takes from you can go up at any time that he feels like raising the income tax rate.

In addition, without the death benefit protection that you secure for your loved ones with a good, solid life insurance policy, you could also be allowing Uncle Sam to take up to half (or more) of the hard-earned assets you intend transfer to your loved ones. With that in mind, the choices you make right now could ultimately have a long-lasting effect.

Maximizing Your Social Security Income

All of the above being said, there are some ways that you can maximize your income from Social Security. In fact, by taking advantage of the right Social Security income strategies for your particular situation, you could end up taking in thousands of additional dollars over time.

If you don't necessarily need your Social Security retirement income benefits right away, you could essentially give yourself a massive "raise" of up to 32% if you wait to take distributions until you are age 70.

Why is that?

Because each year that you hold off on taking distributions between your full retirement age and age 70, your benefit increases by 8%. Let's take a look at how this could work. If, for instance, your full retirement age is 66, and the amount of monthly benefit you were eligible for at that time is $2,000, by waiting until age 67 to start your distributions would be 108% of that, or $2,160 per month.

Using just simple interest, you can see how much more your benefit could grow to if you wait until age 70 – which is the last year that you can receive this delayed income credit. And these figures don't factor in the annual Cost of Living adjustment that you may receive as well.

Age	Monthly Social Security Income

66 (full retirement age)	$2,000
67	$2,160
68	$2,320
69	$2,480
70	$2,640

So, how can less be more?

What if you opt to take Social Security as soon as you're eligible, though, at age 62?

Well, if you go that route, the amount of your monthly benefit will be less than it would be if you wait until your full retirement age. In fact, if you start your benefits early, they will be reduced, based on the number of months you receive them before your full retirement age.

So, if your full retirement age is 66, the reduction of your benefits at age 62 would be 25%. Based on the example above, this reduction could turn your $2,000 per month into just $1,500. Similarly, at age 63, the reduction is approximately 20%, at age 64 it is about 13.3%, and at age 65 the reduction is about 6.7%.

At first glance, that might sound like a pretty drastic reduction in benefits – and it is! But, since none of us has a crystal ball, and we don't know how long we will be on this earth, the reality is that someone who starts benefits at age 62, and passes away at age 65, will at least receive some amount of benefit. And part of something is better than all of nothing!

On the other hand, if you live a nice long life, even with the reduction in your monthly benefits, you could still end up receiving more Social Security income in total by opting to begin your income early and have three or four years' worth of benefit already under your belt prior to your full retirement age.

Because there are many variables that go into the decision about when to start receiving Social Security, it is highly recommended that you sit down and make a well-calculated determination with a professional who is well versed in retirement income.

At FRA Trust, we use a Social Security Life Maximization strategy to help you determine when the right time is for you to start taking your benefits. This can help you with both maximizing your distributions, while at the same time minimizing the taxes you may be required to pay on your Social Security retirement income.

	Pay Through Age 62 - 70	Death Benefit	Income 70 - 84	Total DB & SS	Social Security Alone
Age 62 M	$1,500	$342k	$252k	$594k	$396k
Age 62 F	$1,500	$382k	$252k	$634k	$396k
	Pay Through Age 66 - 70	Death Benefit	Income 70 - 84	Total DB & SS	Social Security Alone
Age 66 M	$2,000	$185k	$336k	$521k	$432k
Age 66 F	$2,000	$208k	$336k	$544k	$432k
	Pay Through Age 70 - 80	Death Benefit	Income at 80	Total DB & SS	Social Security Alone
Age 70 M	$2,600	$524k	$124k	$649k	$436k
Age 70 F	$2,600	$716k	$124k	$840k	$436k

For instance, using the chart above, you can more easily determine the best "mix" of income strategies for you and your specific needs, essentially customizing the way in which various financial "tools" are structured.

*Disclaimer: This is a hypothetical illustration only. Because all situations and objectives can differ, it is best to discuss your specific needs and objectives with a STEP advisor. You can find a STEP advisor by visiting http://fratrust.com/next-step/ or calling 618-632-8558 and requesting a STEP advisor.

What If the Unexpected Occurs?

If there's one thing in life that we can count on, it would be the unexpected. That being the case, there are some "what if's" that you should plan for, just in case. For instance, what if you pass away before you start to receive your Social Security retirement income distributions?

If you have a surviving spouse, he or she could claim Social Security survivor's benefits. In this case, the survivor benefits would be calculated as if the deceased spouse had actually reached full retirement age.

However, unlike the actual retirement benefit – which is based on your highest 35 years of earnings – the survivor benefit amount calculates this figure using fewer years of earnings. This is because the worker's shortened life span is taken into account.

As an example, if a 50-year-old worker - who has enough Social Security work credits to qualify for benefits – passes away, then his or her survivor's benefits would be based on the decedent's highest 23 years of earnings instead.

If you want to get a ballpark figure of how much the survivor's benefits would be, you can take a look at the worker's most recent annual Social Security statement (prior to his or her passing), which shows what they were due to receive at their full retirement age.

This dollar figure would be a close approximation of what a surviving spouse would receive, taking the full retirement benefit amount into consideration. A survivor is allowed to start taking Social Security survivor's benefits as early as age 60 – or even as early as age 50, if the survivor is disabled. However, the amount of the benefit will be reduced if it is claimed prior to the survivor's full retirement age.

A qualified STEP advisor can walk you through how to properly set up income protection in the event of any type of "what if". To find a STEP-trained advisor, just go to: http://fratrust.com/next-step/ or call 618-632-8558 and request a consultation with a qualified STEP advisor.

Chapter 8 Key Takeaways

- Enjoying a retirement that is free from taxes can take both strategic and proactive planning – and this planning must start right now, because the longer you wait, the less likely you are to reap the benefits.
- You may be in a higher income tax bracket during retirement.
- You could be taxed on your Social Security retirement income.
- The tax provisions passed in late 2017 will "sunset" after the year 2025.
- While the monthly dollar amount will be less, taking Social Security income at age 62 could provide you with a higher overall benefit.

Chapter 8 Action Steps

- Determine when the optimal time is to begin taking your Social Security retirement income benefits.

Chapter 8 Questions to Consider

1. True or False: You are likely to have far fewer tax deductions when you reach retirement.

2. With the 2018 tax reform came which of the following changes:
   a. A reduction in the top federal income tax rate
   b. Doubling of the standard deduction
   c. Elimination of personal exemptions
   d. All of the Above

3. While some of the new tax law changes may be beneficial, they are slated to sunset after the year _____.
   a. 2025
   b. 2030
   c. 2035
   d. Never

4. True or False. If you earn more than a stated amount of annual income, a portion of your Social Security benefits could be taxed.

5. Each year that you hold off taking Social Security retirement income benefit distributions between your full retirement age and age 70, your benefit increases by _____%.
   a. 5
   b. 6
   c. 7
   d. 8

Chapter 8 Answers

1. True.

2. With this reform came a number of key changes, including:
- A reduction in the top Federal income tax rate from 39.6% to 37%
- Doubling of the standard deduction
- Elimination of personal exemptions
- Elimination or reduction of many itemized deductions, such as:
    o Deduction for property taxes and / or state / local income taxes limited to $10,000
    o Deduction for alimony
    o Mortgage / home equity interest deduction
- Elimination of the "Please Amendment" limitation on deductions, which means that those who do continue to itemize can do so without limits.

    In addition, the estate tax exemption was increased to just under $11.2 million per taxpayer, with a 40% tax on transfers that exceed the amount of this exemption. Likewise, the gift, estate, and generation skipping tax exemptions increased, per individual, from $5 million to $10 million.

3. While some of these new tax changes may be beneficial, it is important to keep in mind that virtually all of these provisions are only temporary - and they are slated to sunset after the year 2025, reverting back to the previous level. Because of that, it is key that, if you want to take advantage of these tax breaks, it is essential that you do so now rather than later.

4. True.

5. Each year that you hold off on taking distributions between your full retirement age and age 70, your benefit increases by 8%.

Chapter 9: Tying It All Together

Where to Go from Here

"When you invest, you are buying a day that you don't have to work." -- Aya Laraya

Proper planning is a necessity in order to take advantage of tax deductions, as well as tax-reduction and elimination strategies. But just like the old saying goes, "Hope is not a strategy." In fact, even if you have the most in-depth knowledge and the very best of intentions, nothing happens unless or until you take action.

In addition, while we focused on just a couple of tax-free retirement income strategies, there is no such thing as a one-size-fits-all strategy that is right for everyone. With that in mind, it is important that you ensure you're headed in the right direction, and that you will qualify for the plan (or plans) that are best for you and your specific goals.

Our Strategic Tax-free Evaluation Process (STEP) is specifically designed to help you determine where you are already on pace to receive tax-free income, and where any gaps may be. Many of our clients are surprised to learn just how much they could have been at risk of losing to Uncle Sam.

So, if the thought of handing over a large chunk of your retirement income to the government each and every month keeps you awake at night, then it may be time to take a STEP in a different direction!

Will You Qualify for a Tax-Free Retirement Plan?

If you've ever considered becoming the member of an exclusive club, you know that you must first meet the qualification criteria before the doors are open to you. A similar concept holds true for gaining access to the plans that can provide you with tax-free retirement income.

Let's first take a look at the Roth IRA. With this type of account, you will need to be mindful of the income limits, as well as the annual maximum contribution limits.

Roth IRA Income Limits (for 2020)

For single tax filers	Phase-out starts at $124,000 Ineligible at $139,000
For married couples filing jointly and for qualifying widow(er)s	Phase-out starts at $196,000 Ineligible at $206,000

Source: RothIRA.com

Roth IRA Annual Maximum Contribution Limits (for 2020)

Age 49 and younger	$6,000
Age 50 and over	$7,000

Source: RothIRA.com

Roth IRAs can provide you with a powerful way to save for retirement, and to receive income tax-free in the future. But, if you don't qualify for a Roth IRA, don't worry. There may still be a way that you can get around these limits using a strategy called a "backdoor" IRA, where you convert a traditional IRA into a Roth.

A backdoor Roth IRA is essentially a conversion of traditional IRA assets into a Roth – and it can be used by those whose income exceeds the annual contribution maximum. Currently, anyone can convert money that they have put into a traditional IRA – regardless of how much income they earn. And, there is no limit on the amount of money that can be transferred.

If you go this route, there are a couple of items to consider. One is that you will need to pay tax on any of the money from your traditional IRA that has not already been taxed. Because the funds that you move to the Roth from the traditional IRA may count as income, this transaction could put you into a higher tax bracket for the year in which the move takes place.

With that in mind, if you happen to be in a low tax bracket in a given year, that could be a good time to move forward with the conversion. In any case, be sure that you know what your tax ramifications will be prior to moving forward.

The benefit of moving from a traditional IRA to a Roth can far exceed the amount of tax that you pay, though, because income distributions that are taken in the future from the Roth IRA will be received tax-free.[1]

Is a Life Insurance Retirement Plan Right for You?

What about using life insurance as a method of securing tax-free retirement income?

Even though there is a long list of arguments for using life insurance in retirement planning, the truth is that it may not be right and / or it may not work for everyone. One reason for this is because, if you are the insured, you will have to be able to qualify for the policy - and in most cases, this means that you will need to be in relatively good health at the time you apply for the coverage.

In addition, there are many rules and regulations that are related to using life insurance as part of your retirement plan. And if they are not followed, you could end up losing the tax-advantaged status of the policy. Likewise, if you end up taking too much out of the cash value, and the policy lapses, all of the loans will immediately become taxable.

It is also important to ensure that the life insurance policy isn't structured as a Modified Endowment Contract. A Modified Endowment Contract, or MEC, is a type of tax qualification for a life insurance policy that's cumulative premiums exceed federal tax law limits. If this occurs, the taxation structure, as well as the policy's classification, changes.

For instance, if a policy were to become a MEC, the taxation of withdrawals from that policy would be similar to that of a non-qualified annuity. In this case, if the policy holder took withdrawals before turning age 59 1/2, he or she would incur a 10% early withdrawal penalty from the IRS.

So, how do you know whether or not your life insurance policy is a Modified Endowment Contract?

There are three criteria that the policy must meet. First, the policy is entered into on or after June 20, 1988. Second, it must meet the statutory definition of a life insurance policy. And third, the policy must fail to meet the "Technical Miscellaneous Revenue Act (TAMRA) 7-pay test.[4]

This 7-pay test determine whether the total amount of premiums paid into a life insurance policy, within the first seven years, is more than what was required to have the policy considered as "paid up" in seven years. A policy becomes a Modified Endowment Contract when premiums paid into it are more than what was actually needed to be paid within that 7-year timeframe.[5]

There is another key tax-related difference between a regular life insurance policy and a MEC, and that is, unlike traditional life insurance policies, the taxes on gains are considered to be regular income for a MEC withdrawal under the last in, first out (LIFO) accounting methods. In this case, though, the cost basis within a MEC and withdrawals are not subject to taxation.[6]

Given all of that, should you consider adding life insurance to your overall retirement plan?

The answer is that it depends. However, it could be a smart move if you:

- Have the need for life insurance coverage
- Have fully funded all of your other qualified retirement plan options and you would still like to put away some additional tax-advantaged dollars for retirement
- Can overfund the life insurance premiums for at least ten years
- Don't need to begin taking any distributions from the policy for at least 10 years
- Are insurable (although there are ways today to qualify for coverage, even if you have serious health issues)

Because using this type of strategy is somewhat complex, and it requires a careful structuring of the life insurance policy, it is important to discuss your specific goals, objectives, income needs, and time frame with an advisor who has experience in this type of planning.

Taking the Next STEP Towards a Tax-Free Retirement

Regardless of where you are in life right now, it's never too late to analyze your financial plan in order to ensure that you are getting the most that you can out of it - which includes putting more money in your pocket, and less in Uncle Sam's.

Even the difference of netting just a few additional dollars per month in tax-free versus taxable income can truly add up - so taking the time to determine where improvements can be made is well worth the time. And the sooner you do so, the sooner you can start to enjoy the fruits of your labor.

Going about this process on your own, though, can turn out to be detrimental. That being said, there is plenty of additional information available, and ready for you to take advantage of - especially when working with the right advisor like FRA Trust.

All FRA Trust advisors specialize in STEP planning. So, when you work with us, you can be assured that you're getting the most customized advice, based on your specific goals and objectives.

Chapter 9 Key Takeaways

- Planning sooner rather than later can help you to ensure that you're moving in the right direction, and that you qualify for various financial tools like life insurance.
- It is recommended that you work with a financial advisor who is well-versed in tax-advantaged retirement planning.

Chapter 9 Action Steps

- Set up a time to meet with a qualified STEP Advisor by calling (800) 279-9785. Or visit our website at: www.FRATrust.com for more information.

Chapter 9 Questions to Ponder

1. The STEP process stands for _____.
   a. Strategic Tax-free Evaluation Process
   b. Strategies To Evaluate Probate
   c. Strategic Taxation Evaluation Process
   d. None of the Above

2. True or False: There are income limitations that could limit who is eligible to participate in a Roth IRA.

3. True or False: It may be too late to analyze your financial plan in order to ensure that you are getting the most that you can out of it.

4. A _____ is a type of tax qualification for a life insurance policy that's cumulative premiums exceed federal tax law limits.
   a. Index universal life
   b. Modified Endowment Contract
   c. Whole life
   d. None of the Above

5. True or False: Even if you have the most in-depth knowledge and the very best of intentions, nothing happens unless or until you take action.

Chapter 9 Answers

1. The Strategic Tax-free Evaluation Process, or STEP, is specifically designed to help you determine where you are already on pace to receive tax-free income, and where any gaps may be.

2. True.

3. False. Regardless of where you are in life right now, it's never too late to analyze your financial plan in order to ensure that you are getting the most that you can out of it - which includes putting more money in your pocket, and less in Uncle Sam's.

4. A Modified Endowment Contract, or MEC, is a type of tax qualification for a life insurance policy that's cumulative premiums exceed federal tax law limits. If this occurs, the taxation structure, as well as the policy's classification, changes.

5. True.

Chapter 9 Sources

1. RothIRA.com

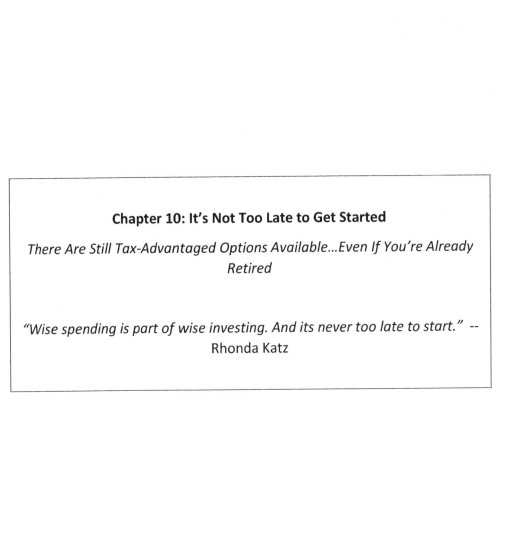

Chapter 10: It's Not Too Late to Get Started

There Are Still Tax-Advantaged Options Available...Even If You're Already Retired

"Wise spending is part of wise investing. And its never too late to start." -- Rhonda Katz

Although we have discussed several viable tax-free retirement income strategies, there may be some readers who fear that it is too late for them because they are already retired. But if you fall into this category, don't worry, because there are still some nice options available for you.

As mentioned in Chapter 5, one nice alternative is the fixed indexed annuity. Like the indexed universal life insurance policy, a fixed indexed annuity can provide you with many of the same advantages, especially as they pertain to growth, safety of principal, and tax-deferred status.

In addition to that, a fixed indexed annuity can also offer you peace of mind in retirement. That's because these financial vehicles can provide you with a guaranteed stream of income for the remainder of your lifetime – regardless of how long that may be. This, in turn, can assure you that you won't run out of income before your "run out of time."

The Many Benefits of Fixed Indexed Annuities

Fixed indexed annuities provide many of the same types of benefits as indexed universal life insurance – except that instead of insuring someone in the case of "dying too soon," these financial products offer income protection for those who essentially "live too long."

Because of their structure, fixed index annuities can offer investors an option that provides them with less risk than being invested in the stock market, yet still with the opportunity to obtain market-like returns.

In other words, this type of annuity offers the opportunity to participate in the market's upside when an underlying market index (or indices) is performing well, but also protects you from downside losses.

These annuities can also provide you with an income stream for life. In addition, you still have control over your money - and you can get to it if you have an emergency and need liquidity.

Although all fixed index annuities are not exactly the same, these financial vehicles do have some common features - many of which can be beneficial to those who hold these products. As with other insurance and financial products, not all fixed index annuities are the same. In fact, far from it. So, if you go the route of a fixed indexed annuity, here are some important criteria to keep in mind and to have a good understanding of before you move forward:

Index-Linked Growth

Similar to index universal life insurance policies, fixed index annuities are also tied to an underlying index such as the S&P 500. Yet, while your funds are tied to the performance of the underlying index, you are not investing directly in the market itself. The nice thing here is that you are typically also guaranteed a minimum rate of return, so if the market performs poorly, your principal is still protected.

With this in mind, make sure that you know what index (or indexes) your money is tracking inside the annuity. In addition, some fixed indexed annuities offer a guaranteed rate of interest for a certain number of years. So, make sure that you are aware of the rate and the term – and any "tradeoffs" (such as surrender periods) before you dive in.

Floor

The floor is the minimum guaranteed rate that is paid to the annuity holder each year. This means that no matter what the underlying index does in a given year, the annuity holder will still receive the amount of the floor.

For example, if you have a floor of 0 percent, and the underlying index that your annuity tracks had a return of negative 15 percent in a given year, your account would receive 0 percent. Therefore, even though you did not gain, your account would not lose a penny.

Here too, depending on the particular annuity you decide on, this guarantee can differ from one annuity to another. And, make sure you know what you have to give up (such as keeping your money in the annuity for a certain period of time) before moving forward.

Reset Feature

The reset feature is the comparison on the index's year-end value to the start of the next year. This calculation determines the interest that you are credited based on the performance of the index and the contract terms.

Also, as previously discussed, there are no market losses credited to your account in an indexed annuity (or indexed life insurance policy's cash value). This can allow you to continue building on your gains, without having to recapture any loss. This is extremely important to keep in mind when comparing the annual return, say, on a mutual fund or stock that may provide you with high returns in some years, but losses to make up for in others.

Tax-Deferred Growth

Although it's been mentioned before, it bears repeating that while your funds are still accumulating inside of the account, they are able to grow on a tax deferred basis. This means that no matter how much the underlying index may increase - in turn, causing your funds to grow in value - you will not be required to pay tax on that growth until the time of withdrawal.

This allows your funds to essentially compound - gains on top of gains, year after year - until you are ready to retire and take the money out of the account. Over time, this can allow your funds to increase substantially.

Taxable versus Tax Deferred Growth Over Time

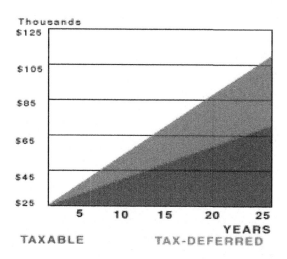

As you can see from the chart above, throughout a time period of 25 years, the power of tax deferred growth can have a tremendous effect on just how much more your savings can grow - even with all other factors being comparable.

Optional Income Riders

Additional income riders can also be added to your fixed index annuity. These can provide more income guarantees of a certain percentage for the time that the underlying market may be stagnant.

The payout of income comes when you begin to withdraw funds from your original investment in the annuity. If you follow the guarantee rules, your income will be guaranteed for the rest of your life.

These riders tend to be somewhat confusing, so before you opt for any type of add-on, make sure that the added premium cost is worth it, based on the benefits that you can receive.

Some Items to Consider Before Committing to a Fixed Index Annuity

There are numerous advantages to owning a fixed index annuity. These include:

- The opportunity for growth that is based on the performance of the underlying index, yet with protection of principal and a minimum rate guarantee
- Tax deferred earnings on growth of your funds that are inside of the annuity account
- No maximum limit on contributions that you can make into the account
- Funds can bypass probate and go directly to beneficiaries while the annuity still has value
- In most states, annuity funds are also protected from creditors
- Lifetime retirement income - guaranteed!

But, while these financial vehicles can offer a long list of advantages, there is a wide variety of fixed indexed annuities being offered in the market place today, and they are not all structured the same way.

So, if you would like to learn more about how a fixed indexed annuity can provide you with tax-advantaged growth, along with a lifetime stream of guaranteed income, contact us at (800) 279-9785 to set up a time to talk.

Chapter 10 Key Takeaways

- Even if you are already retired, it may not be too late to take advantage of various tax-and income-related strategies.
- A fixed index annuity can provide you with an income for the remainder of your lifetime – regardless of how long that may be.

Chapter 10 Action Steps

- Set up a time to discuss your objectives with one of our trained STEP advisors by calling (800) 279-9785.
- Visit our website at: www.FRATrust.com for more information on how to reduce or eliminate taxes from your retirement income.

Chapter 10 Questions to Ponder

1. True or False: Annuities can offer insurance for those who basically "live too long."

2. The _____ is the minimum guaranteed rate that is paid to a fixed indexed annuity holder each year.
   a. Floor
   b. Ceiling
   c. Neither A or B

3. True or False: Because of their structure, fixed index annuities can offer investors an option that provides them with less risk than being invested in the stock market, yet still with the opportunity to obtain market-like returns.

4. True or False: There are no market losses credited to your account in an index annuity.

5. Some advantages to owning a fixed indexed annuity include:
   a. Lifetime retirement income
   b. Protection from creditors
   c. No maximum contribution limits
   d. All of the Above

Chapter 10 Answers

1. True.

2. The floor is the minimum guaranteed rate that is paid to the annuity holder each year. This means that no matter what the underlying index does in a given year, the annuity holder will still receive the amount of the floor.

3. True.

4. True.

5. There are numerous advantages to owning a fixed index annuity. These include:
- The opportunity for growth that is based on the performance of the underlying index, yet with protection of principal and a minimum rate guarantee
- Tax deferred earnings on growth of your funds that are inside of the annuity account
- No maximum limit on contributions that you can make into the account
- Funds can bypass probate and go directly to beneficiaries while the annuity still has value
- In most states, annuity funds are also protected from creditors
- Lifetime retirement income - guaranteed!

Bonus Chapter: The Million Dollar Secret

Using Other People's Money (OPM) to Fund Your Tax-Free Wealth

"It's humbling and enthralling to know your legacy when you're alive." --
Laura Schlessinger

If you're like most people, you probably enjoy getting a good deal – and if you can use other people's money, or OPM, to turbo charge the deal, even better yet!

There are a number of items that most people automatically think about financing. Take, for instance, homes, cars, and businesses. But what about life insurance?

As we have covered extensively, life insurance has many unique uses in both individual and business financial planning. In some situations, the insured, for a whole host of reasons, may require a different method to fund the premium obligations than just simply paying out-of-pocket.

In these situations, a very unique and powerful technique can be used - and that is to borrow the premiums from a bank or specialty lender – or use Other People's Money ("OPM") to fund the premiums. This technique is known as premium financing.

Premium financing has been used for well over thirty years, although it is becoming much more prevalent now, as various marketing participants, including life insurance carriers, have embraced its application and possible benefits.

Primarily utilized by high net worth individuals, the financing of life insurance premiums can enhance standard life insurance planning via three principals. These include:

1) use of leverage;

2) the possibility of positive arbitrage;

3) retaining capital.

Leverage is the concept of using debt for amplifying or increasing the long-term benefits of a given life insurance-based transaction.

Positive Arbitrage is possible when borrowing at a certain interest rate to fund a life insurance policy that may credit back an amount that exceeds the interest rate charged on the loan.

Retained Capital is the concept that insureds/borrowers have superior uses for the monies they would use to fund a life insurance policy. These "retained" assets often will provide a rate of return that is superior to other alternatives, thus providing a net economic benefit to the asset holder.

The combination of these three principals with other aspects of financing offer a compelling solution to individuals that can qualify for such an arrangement and manage the risks that may be associated with financing.

Life Insurance Premium Finance Defined

You can finance your car, you home or your business, so why not finance your life insurance premium?

Life insurance premium financing is defined as any arrangement whereby some or all of the required life insurance premiums are borrowed from a direct lender, specialty company or third-party.

Common loan features typically include the following criteria:

- Loans are secured, fully collateralized through a combination of policy cash surrender value and other lender acceptable collateral
- Wide age applicability
- Numerous life insurance product options
- Variety of loan terms and conditions that can be customized, based on the planning scenario and borrower characteristics.
- The out of pocket funds for supporting the loan can be considerably less than the annual premium obligation in a non-financed situation
- A personal guarantee may be required by the lender

Even though premium financing often minimizes the out of pocket costs, it is still important to note here that there is no such thing as "Free Insurance". Rather, premium finance is a method to fund premiums to support genuine insurance needs for individuals that can effectively use leverage while capitalizing on the possible advantage and accounting for the inherent risks.

Let's take a look at a 45-year-old male who requires an annual premium outlay of $500,000 for ten years to purchase a policy with an initial death benefit of $10 million. By reviewing the illustration below, you can see that even with an accrued loan amount of approximately $7.4M in year 14, his net death benefit is still nearly $3.6 million – and it continues to grow over time.

Example of Premium Financing for Life Insurance Cost Analysis

Male, Age 45, with initial Death Benefit of $10.46 million

Disclaimer: The above is a hypothetical example. All situations and results may differ. Contact FRA Trust for a personalized version.

If you've passed the half-century mark and are on the downhill side of 50, premium financing can still work well for you in terms of using leverage to not only secure an ample death benefit, but also to maximize tax-free retirement income.

For example, in my case, at age 59, a loaned premium of $700,000 for just ten years will lock in a death benefit in excess of $10 million – and, even with an accrued loan after a decade, my death benefit is nearly $11 million.

Take a look at how the premium outlay and the net death benefit after my loan repayment perform over the years – and pay particular attention to how the net death benefit grows to over $16.5 million if I should happen to live to age 100.

Premium Financing for Life Insurance Cost Analysis

Disclaimer: The above is a hypothetical example. All situations and results may differ. Contact FRA Trust for a personalized version.

Net Out-of-Pocket Fees

Age	Year	Policy Loan Amount	5 Yr Loan	10 Yr Loan	15 Yr Loan	Arrangement Fee 0.50%	Stress Test Collateral Amount	Bank Letter of Credit Cost @ 1.00%	Total Annual Fees Payable	Annual Interest Payable	Net Annual Cost Payable	Cumulative Annual Fees Payable
Day 1 Requirements		7,000,000	3,500,000	7,000,000	7,000,000	35,000	103,099	0	0	100,000	100,000	100,000
59	1	7,000,000				35,000	103,099	0	0	100,000	100,000	100,000
50	2					0	178,179	0	0	100,000	100,000	200,000
61	3					0	247,549	0	0	100,000	100,000	300,000
62	4		5yr Accrued Loan 3,621,436			0	245,585	0	0	100,000	100,000	400,000
63	5					0	238,096	0	0	100,000	100,000	500,000
64	6					0	246,133	0	0	100,000	100,000	600,000
65	7					0	248,473	0	0	100,000	100,000	700,000
66	8		10yr Accrued Loan 8,393,614			0	245,255	0	0	100,000	100,000	800,000
67	9					0	236,898	0	0	100,000	100,000	900,000
68	10					0	223,810	0	0	100,000	100,000	1,000,000
69	11					0	0	0	0	0	0	1,000,000
70	12					0	0	0	0	0	0	1,000,000
71	13					0	0	0	0	0	0	1,000,000
72	14			15yr Accrued Loan 0		0	0	0	0	0	0	1,000,000
73	15					0	0	0	0	0	0	1,000,000
74	16					0	0	0	0	0	0	1,000,000
75	17					0	0	0	0	0	0	1,000,000
76	18					0	0	0	0	0	0	1,000,000
77	19			20yr Accrued Loan 0		0	0	0	0	0	0	1,000,000
78	20					0	0	0	0	0	0	1,000,000
79	21					0	0	0	0	0	0	1,000,000
80	22					0	0	0	0	0	0	1,000,000
81	23					0	0	0	0	0	0	1,000,000
82	24			25yr Accrued Loan 0		0	0	0	0	0	0	1,000,000
83	25					0	0	0	0	0	0	1,000,000
84	26					0	0	0	0	0	0	1,000,000
85	27					0	0	0	0	0	0	1,000,000
86	28					0	0	0	0	0	0	1,000,000
87	29			30yr Accrued Loan 0		0	0	0	0	0	0	1,000,000
88	30					0	0	0	0	0	0	1,000,000
89	31					0	0	0	0	0	0	1,000,000
90	32					0	0	0	0	0	0	1,000,000
91	33					0	0	0	0	0	0	1,000,000
92	34			35yr Accrued Loan 0		0	0	0	0	0	0	1,000,000
93	35					0	0	0	0	0	0	1,000,000
94	36					0	0	0	0	0	0	1,000,000
95	37					0	0	0	0	0	0	1,000,000
96	38					0	0	0	0	0	0	1,000,000
97	39			40yr Accrued Loan 0		0	0	0	0	0	0	1,000,000
98	40					0	0	0	0	0	0	1,000,000
99	41					0	0	0	0	0	0	1,000,000
100	42					0	0	0	0	0	0	1,000,000

Is Premium Finance Right for You?

Premium finance is certainly not for everyone, though. In fact, this "exclusive" method of funding one's life insurance premium is typically best utilized by those who have a certain size net worth. In fact, clients must typically meet certain requirements, such as:

- Insurable individuals up to age 70
- Net worth in excess of $5 million
- Adjusted Gross Income (AGI) sufficient to cover standard expenses and debt – including the out-of-pocket obligations
- Individual or corporate borrower who is willing to provide required financial and other personal details for review
- Insured/Borrower with demonstrated capability to collateralize the loan at all times

With that in mind, some of the most prevalent users of life insurance premium financing include:

- Privately held business owners
- High income professionals
- Financial professionals
- Corporate executives
- Public corporations
- Non-profits
- Government entities
- Academic institutions
- Family offices
- Retired, high net worth
- Real estate developers
- Professional athletes

It should be noted that some lenders have developed premium finance for the sub-$5 million net worth client segment. These "new" loan types create options for a once under-served portion of the market.

Types of Loans Used with Premium Financing

The majority of premium finance loans are not made to individual borrowers but rather to an entity such as a(n):

- Irrevocable trust
- Revocable Trust
- Form of business
    - LLC
    - C-Corp
    - S-Corp
    - LLP
- Non-profit entity
- Special Purpose Vehicle (SPVs)

In many cases a professional fiduciary (e.g. trustee) will be involved in the premium financing transaction and will also hold a degree of responsibility for the origination and management of the transaction.

Planning Objectives

Premium financing for life insurance can be used a variety of both common and more advanced planning scenarios. The potential benefits are varied and compelling. Just some of the benefits of life insurance premium financing could include:

- Investment portfolios being better maintained, and in turn providing ongoing asset accumulation or capital growth
- Preserving of current cash flow and liquidity – therefore limiting the reduction in income or savings to pay life insurance premiums
- In most cases (and depending on the timing of the death benefit) the opportunity for generating superior yields when contrasted with full out of pocket premium situations
- Reducing of potential tax liabilities – particularly when combined with other estate planning techniques
- Financing of business protection and / or succession applications (i.e., key person, deferred compensation, "Golden Handcuffs")
- Increasing of life insurance purchasing power whereby insureds may be able to acquire more death benefit with less out of pocket costs than when they are using more traditional premium payment methods

Collateral Required for Premium Financing Transactions

One of the most important aspects of any life insurance premium finance transaction is collateral – which is necessary to initiate and manage the loan over time. It is essential to understand that all loans are 100% secured and collateralized at all times. Typical forms of collateral may include:

- Lender acceptable cash surrender value attributed to the financed life insurance policy – this often represents the primary form of collateral
- Cash, cash equivalents, Certificates of Deposit, other banking products
- Money markets and mutual funds
- Individual equities, fixed income securities, exchange traded funds, other registered investment products
- Cash surrender value of other (non-financed) life insurance policies
- Asset Backed Standby Letter of Credit
- Real estate

There are also some other items to consider as it pertains to life insurance premium financing, such as:

- Collateral obligations will change over time, so the insured/borrower should be prepared for these fluctuations
- The hopeful outcome is that positive arbitrage will provide a situation in which the cash surrender value of the funded life insurance policy is the only form of collateral required – although this is never a guaranteed outcome
- Each lender has different requirements as to acceptable forms of collateral and related procedures

Exit Strategies and Loan Payoff

Premium finance loans are not intended to be in place into perpetuity. Therefore, there are usually defined terms and other conditions that outline repayment and / or the possibility to refinance these loans.

Some of the more common methods of repayment include:

- Use of a side fund or retained capital
- Expected, planned liquidity event (e.g., asset sales)
- Funds from an inheritance
- Policy loans or cash surrender withdrawals
- Death benefit proceeds due to the death of the insured

It is highly recommended that individuals have multiple exit strategies. Working with a professional in the premium financing area is critical, so as to better ensure that the transaction is properly set up, and that the insured/policy owner's objectives are being met.

The Premium Financing Process

Applying for a life insurance policy and making the decision to use premium finance is an involved process. But there are specialists in this field that will facilitate the transaction and guide insureds each step of the way.

If you choose to go the route of financing a life insurance premium, here is what you can expect:

1) Review of Objectives. First and foremost, your objectives will be reviewed. Because all needs are not the same for everyone, it stands to reason that life insurance needs and premiums will also differ.
2) Narrow Down the Type and Amount of Coverage. Once your objectives have been discussed, the next step in the process is to determine the best type of life insurance coverage, as well as the amount of benefit.
3) Decide on Financing as the Funding Method. Provided that the parameters are met with regard to net worth, collateral, and assets, as well as age and health, the next step is to move forward with a premium finance loan.
4) Design the Life Insurance Policy. Today, there are numerous types of life insurance coverage in the market. Therefore, it is a key step in the process to design the coverage, cash value build-up, and other policy parameters to best meet the needs of the insured.
5) Loan Modeling. The loan modeling step will provide a prospective, or hypothetical, analysis of the policy's performance, as well as the cost of the loan.
6) Collateral Review. Next, a review of collateral and "stressing: the transaction – given varying economic and financial conditions – can help in determining how the transaction may perform in different circumstances.

7) Decide on the Borrower. Prior to funding the loan, the borrowing entity must be determined. As mentioned previously, typically – rather than the insured being the actual borrower – a trust or other entity will take on this role.

8) Apply for Coverage. The next step in the process is to fully complete the application for the life insurance coverage. This may entail additional paperwork, depending on the policy and the insurance carrier.

9) Underwriting. The life insurance underwriting process will usually encompass both a medical evaluation of the insured, as well as a financial analysis of the overall transaction.

10) Apply for the Loan. The loan application process will generally require both financial and credit underwriting.

11) Loan Documentation / Execution and Placement of Collateral. Provided that the life insurance policy and the loan are approved, the next step is to actually execute the loan. Doing so will typically require the borrower to put up a certain amount of collateral. There are various forms that this collateral may take, including the cash value of the life insurance policy itself, and / or other types of funds or assets. At this point, the initial funding will usually consist of the initial funding of the first year's premium that is due for the insurance policy.

12) Ongoing Management and Loan Administration. Going forward, once the coverage and the loan are in place, it will require that the policy / coverage and the loan are regularly reviewed, and that any necessary changes be made (if applicable).

Risk Management

Using borrowed monies for funding life insurance is a more advanced technique and it does involve a degree of risk. This is one of the reasons why life insurance premium financing is typically reserved for individuals who meet a specific set of criteria.

As highlighted previously, the lender is fully secured at all times and the borrower is contractually bound to fulfill the terms/conditions of the loan agreement. The borrower should anticipate and plan for variations in the policy performance, interest rates, personal financial changes and macro-economic factors – all of which can influence the borrower's capability to manage the loan.

Given these possibilities, all borrowers taking part in these types of transactions should:

- Use loan models and illustrations that simulate rising interest rates and variation in the buildup of the funded life insurance policy's cash surrender value
- Devise multiple exit strategies
- Use properly trained financial advisors who are working in concert with legal and tax counsel
- Take time during each policy year to analyze the arrangement and plan, in advance, for changes (known and unknown)

Just like the other strategies that we have discussed throughout this book, securing a premium financed life insurance policy is not something that you want to tackle yourself. Rather, it is highly recommended that you work with an insurance or financial advisor who is experienced in this area and who can answer any questions that you may have prior to moving forward.

Due to its complexity in nature, in addition to discussing life insurance premium financing with an insurance or financial professional, it is essential to have a conversation with a qualified tax and legal advisor, as well.

At FRA, we can walk you through all of the steps that are necessary to secure life insurance coverage for both personal and business needs – and we can work with you on obtaining the funds that you need if you opt to finance your premium, which will ultimately leave your personal assets available for other, potentially more lucrative, opportunities.

Bonus Chapter Key Takeaways

- You don't necessarily have to spend your own money when paying the premium on a life insurance policy.
- Premium financing can provide numerous benefits, including leverage, positive arbitrage, and retained capital.

Bonus Chapter Action Steps

- If you require life insurance with a higher amount of death benefit, talk with one of our trained STEP advisors to determine whether financing the policy's premium is right for you.

Bonus Chapter Questions to Ponder

1. The financing of life insurance premiums can enhance standard life insurance planning via which of the following principals:
   a. Use of leverage
   b. The possibility of positive arbitrage
   c. Retaining capital
   d. All of the Above

2. _____ is the concept of using debt for amplifying or increasing the long-term benefits of a given life insurance-based transaction.
   a. Leverage
   b. Arbitrage
   c. Capital retention
   d. None of the Above

3. _____ is possible when borrowing at a certain interest rate to fund a life insurance policy that may credit back an amount that exceeds the interest rate charged on the loan.
   a. Leverage
   b. Positive arbitrage
   c. Retained capital
   d. None of the Above

4. True or False: Life insurance premium financing is defined as any arrangement whereby some or all of the required life insurance premiums are borrowed from a direct lender, specialty company or third-party.

5. True or False: Premium finance loans are intended to be in place indefinitely.

Bonus Chapter Answers

1. Primarily utilized by high net worth individuals, the financing of life insurance premiums can enhance standard life insurance planning via three principals. These include:
   - use of leverage;
   - the possibility of positive arbitrage;
   - retaining capital.

2. Leverage is the concept of using debt for amplifying or increasing the long-term benefits of a given life insurance-based transaction.

3. Positive arbitrage is possible when borrowing at a certain interest rate to fund a life insurance policy that may credit back an amount that exceeds the interest rate charged on the loan.

4. True.

5. False. Premium finance loans are not intended to be in place into perpetuity.

Resources

About FRA

Since FRA was first launched 30 years ago, we have grown to become a leading authority in all aspects of estate and income planning. We regularly deliver high-profile seminars across the United States, where we share our expertise in maximizing the value of your hard-earned assets to benefit you in your lifetime, and your family thereafter.

For more information about FRA and our exclusive STEP planning process, you can visit our website at:

www.FRATrust.com.

You can also contact us directly via phone or email at:

(800) 279-9785

marketing@fratrust.com

FRA is conveniently located in O'Fallon, Illinois, at:

805 W. Highway 50

O'Fallon, IL 62269

What People Are Saying

"Informative. Great follow up completing exactly the documents we needed. The process builds trust and confidence. Most happy about our rep's complete knowledge and professionalism. Working with him made the whole process easy. Now that our estate is protected, a big weight is off our shoulders. Everything was completed as promised and we are completely satisfied."

- Allen & Phyllis Weiss

"The process was smooth; went very well. Clearly you guys were looking out for my best interests. I know I will have peace of mind and comfort. I have referred my family and friends to FRA Trust."

- Barbara Arnett

"We attended a seminar, and everyone seemed to be knowledgeable. Our rep was thorough and charming and made the process quite pleasant. The process was friendly, easy, and thorough. We were surprised at the ease and efficiency of the entire process. We now feel comfortable and secure knowing we have clear plans in place. We have referred several of our friends."

- Glen & Joyce McDaniel

"Your guys knew what they were talking about. They helped me see the necessity of getting this done and showed me the path to follow. Made me feel like I can trust them. Knowing that my estate is protected put my mind to rest. I tell everyone to get it done."

- Jean Bierbaum

"I found the seminar to be very informative, to the point that I wanted to learn more. The sincerity of the speaker was genuine and total honest. The advantages of a trust were clearly presented. I am reminded of the Greyhound commercials, 'Take the bus and leave the driving to us.' The experience was very comforting. I found the cost of setting

up a trust to be very reasonable and worthwhile. I feel very gratified and comforted knowing my estate is protected. If anyone is considering working with FRA Trust, be prepared for a very professional and rewarding experience."

- Kenneth G. Kenney Sr.

"I was referred by a friend and feel very satisfied working with FRA Trust."

- Lillian Dobelbower

"We attended a seminar and felt we were at the right place at the right time. The whole process was smooth. We have worried about getting a plan for a long time and are relieved to have our plan in place. FRA Trust people are very efficient and did a great job explaining things. They took the time to really help us understand the planning and process."

- Matthew & Sandra Kozyak

"The one-on-one process gave us a strong level of confidence in their services. We learned a lot. Knowing that our estate is protected put us at ease; we can relax."

- Neil & Averil Daniels

Disclaimer

This material is intended for education and training purposes only, and it is not intended to be, nor should it be construed as, an offer or solicitation for the purchase or sales of any specific securities, financial services, or other non-specified items. Securities products are sold by prospectuses containing more information about the product's fees, charges and limitations, and can only be offered by a qualified registered representative.

The material and concepts presented here are for informational purposes only and should not be construed as tax or legal advice. Please consult with your personal tax professional or legal advisor for further guidance on tax or legal matters.

All figures provided in this book are for illustrative purposes only and do not reflect an actual investment in any product, nor do they reflect the performance risks, expenses or charges associated with any actual investment. Past performance is not an indication of future performance. Actual results may vary substantially from the figures in the examples provided. All rates of return are hypothetical and are not a guarantee of future performance of any asset, including insurance or other financial products. Higher rates of return have been associated with higher volatility.

Examples of compound interest given in this book are strictly hypothetical and do not represent the past or future performance of any investment. Nor do they reflect any fees and charges associated with investments. It is unlikely that any one fixed rate of return would be sustained over time. Both the return and principal value of investments will fluctuate over time.

Guarantees provided in life insurance policies and annuity contracts are subject to the claims-paying ability of the issuing insurer.

Even though the interest credited to indexed annuity contracts or life insurance policies may be affected by an identified market index, these contracts or policies are not an investment in the stock market or the index and they do not participate in any stock or investment.

Generally, withdrawals from an annuity or a qualified retirement plan before age 59 1/2 are subject to a 10% federal tax penalty.

Generally, interest paid on municipal bonds is tax-free, but not all municipal bonds are exempt from federal and / or state income tax. Some bonds may be subject to capital gains tax at sale. Consult your tax advisor for more information.

A distribution from a Roth IRA generally is income tax-free if (a) it meets all the requirements for a qualified distribution [which include a 5-year waiting period and one of several additional requirements, one being that the distribution is made to a beneficiary on or after the death of the individual], or (b) it is a nonqualified distribution to the extent of after-tax contributions [basis].

For federal income tax purposes, life insurance death benefits generally pay income tax-free to beneficiaries pursuant to IRC Sec. 101(c)(1). In certain situations, however, life insurance death benefits may be partially or wholly taxable. Situations include, but are not limited to: the transfer of a life insurance policy for valuable consideration unless the transfer qualifies for an exception under IRC Sec. 101(a)(2) (i.e., the "transfer-for-value-rule"); arrangements that lack an insurable interest based on state law; and an employer-sponsored policy unless the policy qualifies for an exception under IRC Sec. 101(j).

Distributions such as loans and withdrawals from a life insurance policy can only be made if the policy has been in force long enough to accumulate sufficient value. Loans and withdrawals will reduce charges. If a policy lapses while a loan is outstanding, adverse tax consequences may result. Policy loans are generally not taxable when taken and cash withdrawals are not taxable until they exceed basis in the policy. However, if the policy is treated as a modified endowment contract (MEC) by IRS Sec. 7702A, withdrawals and loans may be taxable when taken to the extent of gain in the contract and may be subject to a 10% federal tax penalty if taken prior to age 59 1/2. Cash distributions associated with benefit reductions, including reductions caused by withdrawals during the first 15 years, may be taxable.

To comply with IRS Regulations, we are informing you of the following: Any discussion or advice regarding tax issues contained in this document is not intended to be used, and cannot be used, to avoid taxpayer penalties. Such discussion or advice was written to support the promotion or marketing of the transaction(s) or matter(s) contained in this document. Anyone reading this document or contemplating a transaction that is discussed in this material should seek advice based on the client's particular circumstances from an independent tax advisor.

The Strategic Tax-free Evaluation Process (STEP) is an exclusive product of FRA. Any copying or duplication of this process without permission from FRA is strictly prohibited.

Glossary of Terms

1035 Exchange - Section 1035 of the Internal Revenue Code sets out provisions for the exchange of similar (insurance related) assets without any tax consequences upon the conversion. If the exchange qualifies for like-kind exchange consideration, income taxes are deferred until the new asset is sold. The 1035 exchange provisions are only available for limited types of assets, which include cash value life insurance policies and annuities.

401(k) Plan - A form of private pension that provides tax advantages.

403(b) Plan - Tax deferred annuity retirement plan that is available to employees of public schools and colleges, and to certain non-profit hospitals, charitable, religious, scientific, and educational organizations.

457 Plan - Non-qualified deferred compensation plans that are available to employees of state and local governments and tax-exempt organizations.

A/B Trust – A type of Revocable Living Trust that is for estate planning purposed, typically by married couples. This strategy uses two trusts – A and B – that are created when the first spouse passes away. The couple's assets are divided into two separate trusts when the first spouse dies, giving each spouse the ability to pass the maximum amount of assets allowed to avoid federal estate taxation.

Accelerated Death Benefits - Some life insurance policies make a portion of the death benefit available prior to the death of the insured. Such benefits are usually available only due to terminal illness or for long-term care situations.

Administrator – An individual appointed by the court for the purpose of managing and distributing a probate estate if the decedent died without having a will.

Annual Exclusion – Each calendar year, individuals are allowed to gift a certain amount of property or assets to an unlimited number of others. In 2020, the amount of the annual gift exclusion is $15,000.

Annuitant - An individual who receives payments from an annuity. The person whose life the annuity payments are measured on or determined by.

Annuity - 1) An obligation to pay a stated sum, usually monthly or annually, to a stated recipient. These payments terminate upon the death of the designated beneficiary. 2) A fixed sum of money payable periodically. 3) A right, often acquired under a life insurance contract, to receive fixed payments periodically for a specified duration. 4) A savings account with an insurance company or investment company, usually established for retirement income. Payments into the account accumulate tax-free, and the account is taxed only when the annuitant withdraws money in retirement.

Automatic Paid-Up Additions (PUAs) - Automatic Paid-Up Additions, or PUAs, are what the policy dividends buy automatically, provided that you choose this as your dividend election. Paid-up additional insurance is available as a type of whole life insurance rider. It essentially allows the policyholder to increase the policy's living benefit, as well as its death benefit, by increasing the policy's cash value. Paid-up additions themselves can also earn dividends, meaning that their value can compound over time.

Automatic Premium Loan (APL) - An automatic premium loan, or APL, is an optional provision in life insurance that authorizes the insurance company to pay from the cash value of the policy any premium that is due at the end of the premium payment grace period. This provision can be helpful for preventing unintentional lapse of the policy.

Base Premium - The base premium in a life insurance policy will purchase the most amount of death benefit possible. (With specially designed whole life insurance policies, more of the premium is allocated to Paid Up Additions (PUAs), which will lessen the amount of life insurance coverage, but increase the amount of money that is in the policy's cash value component).

Basis - An amount usually representing the actual cost of an investment to the buyer. The basis amount of an investment is important in calculating capital gains and losses, depreciation, and other income tax calculations.

Beneficiary - A person who is designated to benefit from an appointment, disposition, or assignment (as in a will, insurance policy, etc.); one designated to receive something as a result of a legal arrangement or instrument.

Bond - A debt of a corporation or government that it acknowledges and agrees to pay to the holder of the bond a certain fixed sum of money on a specified date and interest on that sum in the interim.

Buy-Sell Agreement - An agreement between shareholders or business partners to purchase each other's shares in specified circumstances.

Capital Gains Elimination Trust - See Charitable Remainder Trust.

Capital Gains Tax - An income tax on the profits from the same of a capital asset.

Cash Flow - For purposes of this book, cash flow refers to the movement of money. Generating cash flow is producing and managing income to outweigh expenses. The "flow" in "cash flow" refers to the in and out motion of money - how it flows to and from one's pocketbook.

Cash Value - Permanent life insurance policies provide both a death benefit and a component called a cash value. The cash value earns interest on a tax-deferred basis, and often appreciates. The policy holder may accumulate significant cash value over time, and in some cases, can withdraw or borrow these funds. As long as the policy stays in force, the borrowed funds do not need to be repaid, but interest may be charged.

Charitable Lead Trust - A trust in which a charity is named as the beneficiary for a period of time after which names individuals will succeed as the beneficiaries. These trusts are established to pass along assets that generate income to a charity. The benefit of these trusts is that they enable the grantor to still receive income while protecting the asset from taxes and probate.

Charitable Remainder Annuity Trust (CRAT) - A charitable remainder trust in which the named beneficiaries receive a fixed payment of not less than 5% of the fair market value of the original principal over the course of a specified period, after which the remaining principal passes to a charity.

Charitable Remainder Trust (CRT) - A trust in which the individuals named as beneficiaries retain the income from the trust for a designated period of time, usually the lifetime of the beneficiaries, after which the remainder passes to charity.

Charitable Remainder Unitrust - Charitable remainder trust in which the named beneficiaries receive payments of a fixed percentage, and not less than 5% of the value of the trust assets, as determined annually for a specified period, after which the remainder passes to charity.

Children's Trusts - These trusts are established when the beneficiary is a minor.

Codicil - An instrument in writing that is executed by a testator for adding to, altering, explaining, or confirming a will previously made by the testator. This is executed with the same formalities as a will, and having the effect of bringing the date of the will forward to the date of codicil.

Conduit IRA - An individual who rolled over a total distribution from a qualified plan into an IRA can later roll over these assets into a new employer's plan. In this case, the IRA has been used as a holding account, or conduit.

Decedent - The term decedent refers to a person who has died.

Decreasing Term - A term life insurance policy that features a decreasing amount of death benefit. Decreasing term is well suited to provide for an obligation that decreases over the years, such as a mortgage balance.

Deduction - A deduction is typically used to describe money that is automatically taken from your paycheck; what is being subtracted from your income. Taxes, alimony or child support, insurance, union dues, and charitable are common deductions.

Deferral - A form of tax sheltering in which all earnings are allowed to compound tax-free until they are withdrawn at a future date. Placing funds in a qualified plan, for example, triggers deductions for the current year, and postpones capital gains or other income taxes until the funds are withdrawn. (Not all qualified plans provide for tax deductions, though. Contributions may, however, be excluded from gross income).

Deferred Annuity - An annuity that begins making payments on a specified date if the annuitant is alive at that time.

Deferred Compensation Plan - An employee's earnings that are taxed when received or distributed and not when earned, such as contributions to a qualified pension or profit-sharing plan.

Defined Benefit Plan - A plan that is established and maintained by an employer to provide systematically for the payment of determinable benefits to employees over a period of years after retirement, and usually for his or her lifetime. Retirement benefits under a defined benefit plan are measured by, and based upon, various factors, such as years of service rendered and compensation earned. The amount of benefits and the employer's contributions do not depend on the employer's profits. The employer bears the entire investment risk and it must cover any funding shortfall. Any plan that is not a defined contribution plan is a defined benefit plan.

Defined Contribution Plan - Under ERISA (the Employment Retirement Income Security Act), an employee retirement plan in which each employee has a separate account, funded by the employee's contributions and the employer's contributions (usually in a pre-set amount). The employee is entitled to receive the benefit generated by the individual account.

Dividend - A portion of a company's earnings or profits that are distributed pro rata to its shareholders, usually in the form of cash or additional shares.

Donee – A person who receives a gift.

Donor – A person who makes a gift.

Durable Power of Attorney (DPOA) - An instrument granting someone authority to act as agent or attorney-in-fact for the grantor that remains in effect during the grantor's incompetency. Such instruments commonly allow an agent to make healthcare decisions and financial decisions for someone who has become incompetent.

Dynasty Trust - Also referred to as a generation skipping trust, a dynasty trust allows you to transfer significant sums of cash, tax-free, to beneficiaries who are at least two generations younger than you (which is usually your grandchildren).

Effective Tax Rate - The percentage of total income paid in federal and state income taxes.

Employee Stock Ownership Plan (ESOP) - An ESOP plan allows employees to purchase stock, usually at a discount, that they can hold or sell. ESOPs offer a tax advantage for both employer and employee. The employer earns a tax deduction for contributions of stock or cash used to purchase stock for the employee. The employee pays no tax on these contributions until they are distributed.

Estate - 1) All that a person or entity owns, including both real and personal property. 2) The collective assets and liabilities that one leaves after death.

Estate Plan – The written document setting out an estate owner's instructions for disposition and administration of his or her property at their death, incapacity, or total disability.

Estate Taxes - A tax imposed on property transferred by will or by intestate succession.

Executor - The person selected by the testator to complete the provisions of the testator's will.

Face Amount - The face amount stated in a life insurance policy is the amount that will be paid upon death, or at policy maturity. The face amount of a permanent life insurance policy may change over time as the cash value in the policy increases.

Family Trust - A family trust is also referred to as a credit shelter trust, or a bypass trust. For this trust variation, you write a will in which you bequeath a sum to the trust - up to the maximum figure for the estate tax exemption. The balance you will pass on to your spouse, tax-free. With a family trust, there is also an added bonus in that, once money is placed in it, no matter how much that money grows, it will always be free of estate tax.

Fiduciary - An individual or institution occupying a position of trust. An executor, administrator, or trustee.

Generation Skipping Trust (GST) - A trust that is established to transfer (usually principal) assets to a beneficiary more than one generation removed from the settlor. The transfer is often accomplished by giving some control or benefits (such as trust income) of the assets to a non-skip person, often a member of the generation between the settlor and skip person. This type of trust is subject to generation-skipping transfer tax.

Gift – A transfer of property without receiving some type of benefit in return. The person who makes the gift is not obligated in any way to make the transfer.

Grantor - See Trustor.

Gross Cash Value - The gross cash value is the amount of cash value that you can borrow against. This is your account, and it is both owned and controlled by you.

Guardian - A person or persons named to care for minor children until they reach the age of majority.

Heir - A person who, under the laws of intestacy, is entitled to receive an intestate decedent's property. Loosely, a person who inherits real or personal property, whether by will or by intestate succession.

Illustration - A life insurance illustration, or ledger, is a reference tool used to illustrate how a given life insurance policy underwritten by an insurer is expected to perform over a period of time. The insurance illustration assumes that conditions will remain unchanged over the period of time that the policy is held.

Immediate Annuity - A form of annuity paid for with a single premium that begins making payments back to the policy holder right away.

Income - It may seem fairly obvious, but income is more than the salary you earn. It also encompasses monies that are earned from investments, rental properties, annuities, side jobs, sale of personal property, alimony or child support, cash tips, or any other resources that increase the amount of money you use.

Increasing Death Benefit - In many whole life insurance policies, the death benefit (or face amount) can increase each year.

In-force Policy - An in-force life insurance policy is simply a valid policy. Generally speaking, a life insurance policy will remain in-force as long as sufficient premiums are paid, and for approximately 31 days thereafter (due to the grace period).

Insurability - Insurability refers to the assessment of an applicant's health, and is used to gauge the level of risk the insurer would potentially take by underwriting a policy, and therefore the amount of premium it must charge.

Interest (on borrowed cash value) - This is the amount that the insurance company charges you when you borrow against your policy. When a policyholder takes out a loan, they are not actually borrowing money directly from the policy, but rather borrowing the insurance company's money, and using the cash in the policy as collateral. The interest rate that is charged on borrowed cash value can vary from one insurance company to another. It is, however, oftentimes lower than the amount of interest that is charged by lenders when making big ticket purchases. Also, while paying back this type of loan, interest will continue to accrue on the entire amount of your policy's cash value.

Intestate - A term describing the legal status of a person who dies without a will.

IRA (Individual Retirement Account) - A savings or brokerage account to which a person may contribute up to a specified amount of earned income each year. The contributions, along with any interest that is earned in the account, are not taxed until the money is withdrawn (with a Traditional IRA). Alternatively, the money may be withdrawn tax-free with a Roth IRA. The account holder could incur an additional 10% early withdrawal penalty from the IRS if he or she takes money out of the IRA account prior to turning age 59 1/2.

IRA Rollover - An individual may withdraw, tax-free, all or part of the assets from one IRA, and reinvest them within 60 days in another IRA. A rollover of this type can occur only once in any one-year period. The one-year rule applies separately to each IRA that the individual owns. An individual must roll over into another IRA the same property he or she received from the old IRA.

Irrevocable Life Insurance Trust (ILIT) – A trust whereby a life insurance policy is owned by the trust for the purpose of keeping the proceeds out of an individual's estate, thereby avoiding estate taxation on those proceeds.

Irrevocable Trust - A trust that cannot be terminated by the settlor once it is created.

Inter Vivos Trust - A trust that is created by you and take effect during your lifetime.

Interest (on borrowed cash value) - This is the amount that the insurance company charges you when you borrow against your policy. When a policyholder takes out a loan, they are not actually borrowing money directly from the policy, but rather borrowing the insurance company's money, and using the cash in the policy as collateral. The interest rate that is charged on borrowed cash value can vary from one insurance company to another. It is, however, oftentimes lower than the amount of interest that is charged by lenders when making big ticket purchases. Also, while paying back this type of loan, interest will continue to accrue on the entire amount of your policy's cash value.

Intestate - Of or relating to a person who has died without a valid will.

Joint Ownership – The situation where two or more people own the same piece of property together. There are a number of ways property can be jointly owned, including as joint tenants, tenants in common, tenants by the entirety, or other legally defined relationships.

Joint Tenancy – When two or more people take title to the same property and simultaneously each owns 100% of the property, or has full rights to the property. At the death of one joint tenant, his or her share will immediately transfer to the ownership of the survivor(s).

Keogh Plan - A tax-deferred retirement program that is available to those who are self-employed.

Legatee - One who has been named in a will to take personal property; one who has received a legacy or bequest.

Life Estate – An individual has the benefits of a property during their lifetime, however, they do not own the property and therefore when they die, the property is thus not included in their estate.

Life Insurance - A contract between an insurance policy holder and an insurer, where the insurer promises to pay a designated beneficiary a sum of money (the benefits) upon the death of the insured person.

Life Insurance Retirement Plan (LIRP) - A tax efficient way for high income individuals to supplement their retirement income by taking advantage of the tax treatment of a variety of life insurance products.

Life Settlement - A life settlement occurs when a person sells his or her life insurance policy to a third party for an amount that is less than the full amount of the death benefit, but typically more than the cash value. The buyer becomes the new owner and

/ or beneficiary of the life insurance policy, and they will also pay future premiums that are due, and will collect the death benefit when the insured dies.

Living Trust – A type of revocable trust that is used in estate planning in order to avoid probate, help in situations of incompetency, and allow smooth management of assets after the death of the grantor or person who established the trust. The trust can be effective in eliminating or reducing estate taxes for married couples.

Living Will – A document that defines your "right to die." This document typically states that you do not want to have your life artificially prolonged by modern medical technologies.

Manual Paid-Up Additions - Manual paid-up additions are cash payments that can be added on an optional basis. They act similar to an automatic paid-up addition. There are some insurance companies that are more flexible with this option than others.

Marital Deduction – Married couples are allowed to pass to their spouse an unlimited amount of assets upon the first spouse's death without being subject to estate taxation.

Modified Endowment Contract (MEC) - A Modified Endowment Contract, or MEC, is a special type of life insurance under federal income tax law. The law prescribes a test that is intended to differentiate between policies that are purchased primarily for certain tax advantages, versus policies that are purchased primarily for the death benefit protection.

Money Purchase Plan - A Money Purchase Plan has contributions that are a fixed percentage of compensation and are not based on the employer's profits. For example, if the plan requires that contributions be 10% of the participant's compensation, the plan is a Money Purchase Plan. With this type of plan, the employer is committed to making contributions each year, even if the employer has no profits or is experiencing cash flow problems. Employee contributions are limited to 25% of compensation. Employer contributions are also limited to a set maximum.

Mortality - Mortality is the risk of death of a given individual, based on factors such as age, health, gender, and lifestyle.

Multigenerational IRA - Also referred to as an Extended IRA or Stretch IRA. A term used to refer to an IRA that allows the first generation beneficiary to designate a successor beneficiary (or successor beneficiaries) of an inherited IRA, and for the IRA to be passed on to a succession of beneficiaries over the life expectancy of the first generation beneficiary. As of January 1, 2020, based on provisions of the SECURE Act, non-spouse

IRA beneficiaries are required to withdraw all assets from an inherited IRA account within 10 years. (There are no required minimum distributions within those ten years, however, the entire balance must be distributed after the 10th year).

Net Taxable Estate – The net taxable estate or net value is the total or gross value of the estate less liabilities, expenses, and other deductions that are allowed by the tax laws. The result is the value of the estate upon which the federal estate tax will be levied.

Owner - The owner of a life insurance policy is the person who pays the policy's premiums, and is the only person who can borrow against the cash value. The owner and the insured can be one in the same, but they do not have to be.

Paid Up Additions - Paid-up additions are additional insurance that is available as a type of whole life insurance policy rider. This rider allows the policyholder to increase the policy's living benefit, as well as its death benefit, by increasing the policy's cash value. Paid-up additions themselves can also earn dividends, meaning that their value can compound over time. Paid-up additions may be either automatic or manual.

Personal Property – Property other than real estate (land and permanent structures on the land). Cars, furniture, securities, bank accounts, and animals are all examples of personal property.

Policy - A contractual arrangement between an insurer and an insured, that describes the terms and conditions of a life insurance contract.

Policy Loan - A life insurance policy owner can borrow from the cash value component of many permanent life insurance policies, for virtually any reason. Any policy loans that are outstanding at the time of the insured's death will be deducted from the death benefit paid to the policy's beneficiary.

Portfolio - A complete list of all of your investments.

Power of Attorney – Legal document that grants another individual the authority to manage the financial affairs of another. This document becomes invalid when the individual dies or becomes incompetent, unless it is deemed as a durable power of attorney.

Premium - The monthly, quarterly, or annual payments that you make to an insurance company that go into your account and that also pay for the insurance policy's death benefit. Premiums don't necessarily have to come directly out of your pocket throughout the life of the policy. The policy's dividends and / or funds from the cash value may be used for paying the premium.

Private Pension - A pension plan that is established either through your employer or on your own. These plans may or may not qualify for tax advantages. Private pensions differ from public pensions, which are provided to government employees.

Probate - The process whereby the probate courts divide the estate of a deceased person among the creditors and heirs.

Pension - A fixed sum that is paid regularly to a person or dependents following retirement by a private employer or the U.S. Government.

Public Pension - A pension plan that is provided to various government employees.

Qualified Retirement Plan - A retirement plan established through your employer that meets the requirements for tax breaks.

Reduced Paid-Up (RPU) Policies - Reduced paid-up life insurance can allow for the continuation of the coverage without having to pay additional premiums. However, the face amount (death benefit) on the policy will typically be reduced.

Required Minimum Distribution (RMD) - An individual must start receiving distributions from a qualified plan by April 1st of the year following the year in which he or she turns age 72. Subsequent distributions must occur by each December 31st. The minimum distributions can be based on the life expectancy of the individual or the joint life expectancy of the individual and the plan's beneficiary.

Revocable Trust – A trust which can be amended or revoked by the person(s) who established the trust.

Rider - A life insurance policy rider is an amendment to the standard policy that expands or restricts the policy's benefits. Common riders include a disability waiver of premium and a children's life coverage rider.

Roth IRA - A Roth IRA is an individual retirement account that offers a valuable tax break - tax-free income in retirement. Because of that, the money that goes into a Roth IRA is after-tax money.

SECURE ACT – The Setting Every Community Up for Retirement Enhancement (SECURE) Act was signed into law on December 19, 2019, by President Donald Trump, and took effect on January 1, 2020. This legislation pushes back the age at which retirement plan participants must begin taking required minimum distributions, from 70 ½ to 72. It also eliminates the stretch IRA as a strategy for non-spouse IRA and 401(k) beneficiaries. In addition, the SECURE Act allows many part-time workers to participate in employer-sponsored retirement plans, and makes it easier for small business owners to set up "safe harbor" retirement plans that are easier to administer and less expensive.

Settlor – A person who establishes a trust. The term settler is used interchangeably with the terms "trustor" and "grantor."

Spousal IRA - An individual can set up and contribute to an IRA for his or her spouse. This is called a spousal IRA, and it may be established if certain requirements are met. In the case of a spousal IRA, the individual and spouse must have separate IRA accounts. A jointly owned IRA is not permitted.

Succession Planning - Planning for a business to pass to the next generation of owner / managers.

Surrender Value - When a life insurance policy owner surrenders his or her permanent life insurance policy to the insurance company, he or she will receive the surrender value of that policy in return. The surrender value is the cash value of the policy plus any dividend accumulations, plus the cash value of any paid-up additions, minus any policy loans, interest, and applicable surrender charges.

Tax Credit - An income tax credit directly reduces the amount of income tax paid by offsetting other income tax liabilities.

Tax Deduction - A reduction of total income before the amount of income tax payable is calculated.

Tax Deferred - The term tax deferred refers to the deferral of income taxes on interest earnings until the interest is withdrawn from the investment. Some vehicles or products that enjoy this special tax treatment include permanent life insurance, annuities, and investments that are held in IRA accounts.

Tax Sheltered Annuity (TSA) - Tax deferred annuity retirement plan that is available to employees of public schools and colleges, and to certain non-profit hospitals, charitable, religious, scientific and educational organizations.

Taxable Estate – The portion of an estate that is subject to federal estate taxes or state death taxes. Technically, all of an estate is subject to federal estate taxes, but because of the unified credit, only estates with a value over the exemption equivalent amount actually have to pay any estate taxes.

Term Life Insurance - Term life insurance is a type of life insurance coverage that pays out a death benefit if the insured dies while the policy is in force - which is typically a set period of time. Term life insurance policies do not have cash value and must be renewed periodically as dictated by the insurance contract.

Testamentary Trust - A trust that is created through a will and that becomes effective at the testator's death.

Testator - A person who, at death, leaves a valid will.

Transfers of Assets or Spend-down - This practice is prohibited for purposes of establishing Medicaid eligibility. Applies when assets are transferred, sold, or gifted for less than they are actually worth by individuals in long-term care facilities or who are receiving home and community-based waiver services, by their spouses, or by someone else who is acting on their behalf.

Trust - A legal agreement in which the trustor places assets in the possession of a trustee for the benefit of the trust beneficiary.

Trustee - The person, professional, or institution who manages the assets of the trust under the terms of the trust declaration.

Trustor - A person who intentionally creates a trust. Also known as a settlor or grantor.

Underwriting - Underwriting helps to properly price an insurance policy. Insurance underwriters use computer programs and actuarial data to determine the likelihood and the magnitude of a claims payout over the life of the policy.

Underwriting Class - Underwriting class, also often referred to as risk class, refers to insureds who exhibit similarities that allow them to be grouped together. Insurance companies need to know the likelihood that taking on, or underwriting, a new policy for a new insured will be a profitable endeavor. It also helps with determining the amount of premium that should be charged for coverage. Most life insurance companies have three primary risk classes that individuals may be placed into. These are Preferred, Standard, and Substandard. Those who are in the Preferred class will tend to have lower premium rates because they are the least risky to insure. The Standard class is considered to be the most typical, with those in this group paying "average" premiums for their coverage. The Substandard class is considered to be the riskiest for the insurance company, and because of that, the premium that is charged will typically be in the higher range. Within each of these three primary underwriting classes can be numerous sub-categories as well.

Unified Credit – A tax credit is given to each person by the IRS to be used during his or her life or after his or her death. The tax credit equals the amount of tax (gift or estate) which is assessed on the exemption equivalent value of property. It is considered to be the "unified" credit because it applies to both gift taxes and estate taxes and results from the IRA's effort to unify these two taxes or make them consistent.

Universal Life Insurance - An adjustable life insurance policy that provides both a death benefit and an investment component called cash value. The cash value earns interest at rates that are dictated by the insurer. The policy holder may accumulate cash value on a tax deferred basis. They may also be able to withdraw or borrow the cash value funds, without the need to pay taxes if they borrow. (Although tax may be required if the policy is surrendered). As long as the policy remains in force, the borrowed funds do not need to be repaid. However, interest may be charged to the cash value account. Premiums are also adjustable, within certain guidelines, by the policy owner.

Unlimited Marital Deduction – The tax law that allows a person to give an unlimited value of property as a gift, or leave an estate of unlimited value to his or her spouse without a gift or estate tax being assessed.

Variable Universal Life Insurance - A policy that provides both a death benefit and an investment component called a cash value. The owner of the policy invests the cash value in sub-accounts that are selected by the insurance company. The policy holder may accumulate cash on a tax deferred basis, and may borrow the funds without paying tax on the borrowed gains. (Although tax may be required if the policy is surrendered). As long as the policy remains in force, the funds do not need to be repaid. However, interest may be charged to the cash value account.

Viatical Settlement - A viatical settlement occurs when a person who has a terminal or chronic illness sells his or her life insurance policy to a third party for an amount that is less than the full amount of the death benefit. The buyer becomes the new owner of the policy, and also the beneficiary. The buyer will collect the death benefit when the insured dies.

Waiver of Premium - A waiver of premium rider is a clause in an insurance policy that will waive the policyholder's obligation to pay any additional premiums if he or she becomes seriously ill or disabled, and is unable to work and make the premium payments. Not all insureds are able to qualify for this, however, if it is available on a life insurance policy, it can be a beneficial addition.

Whole Life Insurance - A type of permanent life insurance that provides both a death benefit and a cash value component. The policy is designed to remain in force for a lifetime. Premiums remain level and the death benefit is guaranteed. Over time, the cash value grows on a tax deferred basis. While the premiums for a whole life insurance policy may start out higher than that of a comparable term life insurance policy, over time the level premium will eventually become smaller than the ever-increasing premium for term life insurance coverage.

Will – A legal document that states the intentions of a deceased person concerning the distribution of his or her assets and property, as well as the management of his or her affairs following their death. State law typically dictates the legality of a will.

Made in the USA
Monee, IL
02 February 2020

21214338R00098